ORC[illegible] CONVERSATIONS

PREPARING GROUPS TO TAKE ON ADAPTIVE CHALLENGES

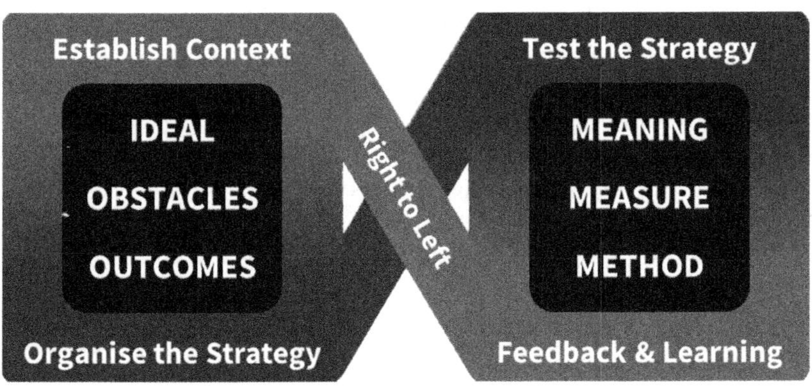

MIKE BURROWS

BMI Publishing
Bushe-Marshak Institute for Dialogic Organization Development
3898 Trenton Place, North Vancouver, BC Canada V7R 3G5
https://B-M-Institute.com

Library and Archives Canada Cataloguing in Publication
Title: Organizing conversations : preparing groups to take on adaptive challenges / Mike Burrows.
Names: Burrows, Mike, 1965- author.
Series: BMI series in dialogic organization development.
Description: Series statement: BMI series in dialogic organization development; 9 | Includes
bibliographical references.
Identifiers: Canadiana 20240388984 | ISBN 9781777184674 (softcover)
Subjects: LCSH: Organizational change; 9. | LCSH: Conversation. | LCSH: Leadership.
Classification: LCC HD58.8 .B856 2024 | DDC 658.4/06—dc23

ISBN: 978-1-7771846-7-4
Imprint: BMI Publishing
Page design: Self-publish.ca

Contents

PART TWO: MANAGING THE INQUIRY PROCESS AND ORGANIZING ITS OUTPUTS

PART THREE: GENERATIVE PROCESSES

Foreword by the Series Editors

The term Dialogic Organization Development was first used in a 2009 article published in *The Journal of Applied Behavioral Science*. In that article, we described how organization development had evolved and contrasted it with the original form of OD, which we labeled Diagnostic OD. We were unhappy with how OD textbooks treated the newer premises and practices as if they fit the earlier model. We wanted to create a space for people to think about, research, develop, and discuss these newer approaches to change. This book series is a continuation of that ambition and purpose.

Dialogic OD is a still-developing mindset (rather than a set of specific methods). It is rooted in two key intellectual movements that influence all social sciences: how social reality is constructed, maintained, and changed by how we talk (post-modernism) and how social systems emerge and self-organize without leadership direction or a plan (complexity science). We have written several articles and book chapters about this, and readers of this book (and all books in the series) are encouraged to access our website, www. B-M-Institute.com. Most of our writings and those of others are available there for free. The articles and book chapters on the website provide a general overview of Dialogic OD theory, how it is the same and different from Diagnostic OD, and basic ideas about leadership, consulting, change, and creating great organizations embedded in Dialogic OD.

Since 2005, we have devoted time and attention to conceptualizing and explaining Dialogic OD. Now, we focus on encouraging presentations of specific dialogic practices applicable to all change methods and approaches. Each book in this series is a short, focused, and practical exploration of one topic to expand the theory and practice of Dialogic OD. We hope you enjoy the books. We welcome proposals for further volumes.

If you are relatively new to this set of ideas, you can download and read the free "Companion Booklet to the BMI Series in OD" by visiting www.b-m-institute.com website.

July 2019
Gervase R. Bushe
Robert J. Marshak

Acknowledgments

The engagement model underpinning this book has been a collaborative effort. Its early development owed a great deal to Dragan Jojic (UK), Karl Scotland (UK), Andrea Chiou (US and France), and Steven Mackenzie (UK); their input and influence continue into the present. Latterly, I would add Kert Peterson (US and Canada), Patrick Hoverstadt (UK), Philippe Guenet (UK), Jonathan Sibley (US), Andreas Wittler (Germany), Tom Ayerst (UK), Matthew Dodwell (UK), Kjell Tore Guttormsen (Norway), and Teddy Zetterlund (Sweden).

Beyond those names, leaders prominent in communities that intersect with Agendashift's: Gervase Bushe and Bob Marshak (Canada & US, Dialogic and Generative Organization Development), Dave Snowden (UK, Cynefin), Simon Wardley (UK, Mapping), and Daniel Mezick (US, OpenSpace Agility).

For this book in particular, I must first express my thanks to Gervase in his role as series editor, not only for inviting me to write this book, but for his repeated challenges to make explicit the thinking that underlies the practice here described. On more than one occasion I had no ready answer, and his probing has had benefits therefore that go beyond the book. I am grateful also to Gary Wong (Canada), Sarah Lewis (UK), Bülent Duagi (Romania), and Adalbert (Adi) Rajca (Germany).

Finally, my wife Sharon has endured the writing of four books now and has learned to recognize the signs even before writing has started. Through it all, she has been a constant source of support and encouragement. Thank you, Sharon, and thank you all!

Mike Burrows
May, 2024

Introduction

The models and processes in this book emerged from a frustrating personal experience that I found to be all too common—being asked to help a group become more *Agile* or *Lean*, only to discover that many in the room had no idea why they were there, what the purpose of the change was, or why the change was needed. To those people, I was there not to help but to impose.

Trying to impose new ways of organizing on people with no say in what happens is rarely successful; here, it was both dissonant and ironic. Dissonant, because we were telling people that we wanted them to take more ownership and responsibility for their work, yet gave them no input into that change. Ironic because the Agile manifesto's first rallying cry of "*People and interactions over processes and tools*" (agilemanifesto.org, 2001) was ignored.

Means create ends. If we want people to take more responsibility for their work, we must use change processes consistent with that goal. By that same token, why not start with the change process if we want creativity, collaboration, and innovation?

Too often, a change in organizing—changing how people relate to (among other things) each other, their work, and the means of doing that work—is decided upon by senior managers and imposed on those who will have to change. The failure rate of this approach to change is well documented (Eaton, 2010; Mosadeghrad & Ansarian, 2104; Towers Watson, 2013). Why, then, do leaders keep doing it?

Firstly, they begin with the assumption that there is a best way to organize and that experts (often experts from outside the organization) know better than those who do the work. There are several reasons to conclude that this assumption is wrong. Dialogic OD shows there are infinite ways to organize ourselves, limited only by our imagination and the agreements we can make among ourselves (Cooperrider & Srivastva, 1987).

Secondly, we've found that how people make meaning of any change is critical to its success (Barrett et al., 1995; Bushe & Marshak, 2015). Attempts to implement change run into the prevailing narratives and assumptions among the current workforce. For example, telling supervisors they should now engage employees in group problem-solving when those supervisors believe they are mainly assessed on employee productivity will fail.

Thirdly, the paradoxical nature of organizing ensures that any solution to a problem of organizing will inevitably create a new problem (Bushe & Nagaishi, 2018; Van de Ven, 1986). Organizing people is rife with "polarities" (Johnson, 2020)—competing and even paradoxical demands. We want efficiency and control, and we want innovation and flexibility. We want collaboration and self-responsibility, and diversity and constructive conflict. We want attention to what's going on outside the organization and attention to what's going on inside the organization. Dozens of such polarities have been identified (e.g., Cameron & Quinn, 2011; Johnson, 2020; Smith & Berg, 1987), and organizing is best viewed as a never-ending series of adjustments between opposing but interdependent needs. For example, organizations centralize to increase coordination and control until that becomes too stifling and then decentralize to increase flexibility and innovation until that becomes too inefficient and then return to centralizing. And on it goes.

Consequently, what works in one organization may not work in another. We see this failure repeatedly in attempts to copy successful innovations in work practices without revising them for fit. Only the simplest problems are amenable to "*best practices*"—see the sensemaking framework *Cynefin* (Snowdon & Boone, 2007)—and how people will organize themselves to be more effective is not a simple problem. Neither is it reasonable to assume that any solution will endure indefinitely.

And so to *Organizing Conversations*, a consciously ambiguous title in a field necessarily ripe with ambiguity. Its themes are:

- Dialogic patterns—models, routines, and strings of exercises that organize a range of powerful conversational tools and give structure and direction to exploratory dialog

- Participatory tools for organizing the outputs of such *inquiry*, dealing respectfully with its quantity, its diversity, and, yes, its ambiguity
- Patterns for *generative conversations*—conversations designed to yield solutions that people are motivated to act on
- Patterns for integrating and sustaining the above, seeing that as an issue of organization as much as a process

The title is also a nod to Karl Weick's *The Social Psychology of Organizing* (1979, 1969), which taught me to prefer 'organizing' over 'organization'. That more dynamic and relational alternative really helps.

Where this book comes from

Let me start not quite at the beginning. Here, unedited, is an exchange between series editor Gervase Bushe and myself. Notice how the conversation works:

Gervase: I'd like to get a statement of your theory of action for creating generative conversations. Complete this sentence: In order to design events that produce generative conversations among a group of people you have to…

Mike: In order to design events that produce generative conversations among a group of people you have to sustain their motivation to ask and answer questions not previously considered in their context, and to which the answers may be both many and potentially surprising (including to the event's designer, who neither mediates in every conversation nor prescribes their conclusions). The strength of that motivation comes from a combination of purpose, context, trust in the process on the day, and confidence (or at least hope) for what will follow.

Gervase: Interesting. Now, to sustain their motivation to ask and answer questions not previously considered in their context, you have to...

Mike: To sustain their motivation to ask and answer questions not previously considered in their context, you have to:

connect conversations to their individual and collective

aspirations (perhaps not previously expressed) and to their everyday reality

reveal enough of the design to give confidence that these conversations are going somewhere and will lead to something, the detail of the process unfolding at the right times and with allowance for adjustment

make progress at a rewarding rate—fast exploration when that is what's needed, slowing down when the payoff is in the deeper reflection or reconsideration—choosing the tools accordingly

Gervase: Excellent. And to create confidence (or at least hope) for what will follow, you have to...

Mike: To create confidence (or at least hope) for what will follow, you have to prepare the ground early for future activities. This includes:

creating the positive expectation that learning—even more than results in those initial stages—will be accounted for, and

maintaining a clear separation between solutions and outcomes, emphasizing the latter and making room for the people closest to the problem to participate

Three prompts—not quite questions, but close enough—and three answers, covering a lot of ground. And with that short conversation, this book was born.

Let's see how that conversation worked. Its most striking feature is Gervase's repeated use of this prompt:

To <*some words previously used by me*>, you have to...

Technically speaking, this is an example of a *generative process*: repeatedly applying some defined procedure to produce new results, often taking the output of one such application as the input to the next. What's remarkable is the power of such a process to produce things that have never been said before—and perhaps not even thought before. Consciously resisting the natural urge to inject their thoughts into the conversation, Gervase's restraint enhances insight and creativity.

Another important feature of this conversation is Gervase's setup:

> "I'd like to get a statement of your theory of action for creating generative conversations. Complete this sentence: ..."

Unlike the following prompting, the setup was very much in his own words, including a couple of thought-provoking phrases: *"theory of action"* and *"generative conversations."* It's not hard to imagine Gervase holding a similarly structured conversation with a different setup on an entirely different topic. No less importantly, he could start the same conversation with someone else—or even with me on a different day—and get very different results. Here is a recognizable, repeatable, and useful structure, a *pattern*.

Not all of what made that conversation work was explicit. Implicitly, Gervase and I had enough context and language in common that much didn't need to be said, and what was said could be said efficiently. Moreover, we had a common purpose: the prospect of this book.

Some of that context and purpose were created in previous conversations; the rest we already had in common. Unremarkable, perhaps, but as I have suggested, not to be taken for granted either! To apply a pattern effectively, you must know how to use it and when. And sometimes, it takes real effort to create the conditions in which it will be successful.

Rewind the clock to 2016, and I would not have known what to do with Gervase's setup. It would have been a short conversation indeed! But the intent was certainly there. I was highly dissatisfied with how conventional, prescriptive, rollout-based approaches to change were applied to Agile transformation with no hint of irony. For too many people, their first experience of Agile was about having processes and tools imposed upon them and then finding the results no less frustrating than that experience. I found myself in the strange position of being a recognized author in the Lean-Agile community but drifting to its edges, an indication of both my dissatisfaction and my determination to find some better approaches.

Step 1—and one of the best things I ever did—was to use my community standing to gather under the Agendashift brand a helpfully diverse community of people who shared my dissatisfaction and the positive desire to do something about it. Client by client, workshop by workshop, even meetup by meetup, we experimented, shared, mashed up, refined, connected to theory, and planned the next wave of experimentation.

By 2018, Agendashift was defined well enough for a book, and it continued to develop quickly enough for a second edition in early 2021. Meanwhile, it has been used worldwide by people close and not so close to its key contributors, demonstrating that it is not just repeatable and transferrable but independently reproducible, too.

One model to the tune of another

As part of our quest to anchor it in appropriate theory, between those two editions, I was introduced to *Dialogic Organization Development* (Bushe & Marshak, 2015). I was thrilled to discover that Agendashift could already be described as a dialogic approach. And it got better: Gervase's 2020 book *The Dynamics of Generative Change* arrived just in time for the *Agendashift* second edition to include a reconciliation with the Generative Change Model (see figure 12). The fit seemed remarkably good; despite being developed independently, Agendashift could reasonably be described as implementing the model.

I don't mind admitting that when I first reconciled Agendashift with the Generative Change Model, I did it as a kind of validation, and I would be the first to acknowledge that I understood the model on my own terms. But there was some real learning, too: it changed my understanding of Agendashift and has made a noticeable impact on its continued development.

This book provides a set of patterns, or templates, for helping a group of people identify, act on, and learn from changes in how they work together. **Outcomes before solutions** is the most basic, foundational pattern. Here, I will define solutions as concrete changes chosen for implementation, while outcomes are what we want solutions to accomplish. Agile, Total Quality Management (TQM), digital, or artificial intelligence are solutions, but for what? To what end? What outcome or outcomes are we trying to accomplish?

While leaders are responsible for framing and highlighting the challenges that require a change in how we work together, the people best positioned to identify the outcomes needed are those who work closest to those challenges. Not just their input but their ownership is essential, and the conditions for that are created by dialog—exploring their constraints and opportunities, motivations and interests, beliefs, assumptions, and narratives. What dialogic change processes have repeatedly shown is that change is much more likely to be successful if we ask those who must change what they think is meaningful and possible (Hastings & Schwartz, 2022).

The patterns I describe in this book can be used with any group at any level of organization, whether it's a senior leadership team, teams engaged directly in product development or service delivery, a multilevel large group process, or anything in between. Some of the best groups I've worked with have had representation from every level. On one occasion, the new joiner sat next to a member of the C-suite, and both enjoyed a productive time.

We have established that we need people's active participation in the change process, lest its contradictions fatally undermine the endeavor. Accordingly, much of this book describes participatory exercises and the sources that inspire them. Many of these exercises are open source—published under a Creative Commons CC-BY-SA license that encourages adaptation—and their supporting materials are available at agendashift.com/resources.

These exercises are documented in my book *Agendashift: Outcome-oriented Change and Continuous Transformation (2nd edition 2021); some also appear in Right to Left: The Digital Leader's Guide to Lean and Agile*. More recently, they were adapted for use in Leading with Outcomes (leading-with-outcomes.com), the Agendashift Academy's leadership development curriculum.

Despite that former book's detailed reconciliation between its underlying model and Gervase Bushe's Generative Change Model, writing for the BMI Series in Dialogic Organization Development has been challenging and learningful. I am grateful for the opportunity to clarify and make explicit things I had previously left unsaid. For example:

1. Many leaders—including a fair few facilitators—are unduly anxious to drive conversations toward convergence, resolution, and decision. But as good *hosts*, is that what's needed now with this group? Sometimes, decisions are required to move things forward, but often, it would be more effective to hold a space where what emerges becomes the kernel for something the whole group truly owns.

2. Not only is it helpful to distinguish decision-making (whose purpose is not to create options but to eliminate them) from

other stages or modes of conversation, I have also found it helpful to respect the distinction between *inquiry* and *generative conversations*. While inquiry at its best does have a generative quality—surfacing previously unarticulated thoughts and perhaps integrating a range of different perspectives in ways that prompt further ideas—that kind of dialog is often a step or two removed from creating ideas that people are motivated to act on.

Overview of the book

Broadly, this book connects those two kinds of dialog—*inquiry* (chapters 1-3) and *generative conversations* (chapters 6 and 7)—such that each feeds the other. Bridging those, chapters 4 and 5 are devoted respectively to configuring the inquiry and organizing its output to promote generative conversations and maximize feedback from the resulting action.

To use a different lexicon, you could say that I am integrating the development and pursuit of strategy. Please don't be put off by the word *strategy* here—this is not strategic planning in the traditional sense. Instead, I mean strategy as a way to accomplish a purpose. Use outcomes not to set targets or to prescribe solutions but:

1. As focal points (or *affordances*) that, by their quantity and diversity, invite action on a broad front.
2. As indicators of meaningful progress away from the status quo.
3. As overarching goals that organize the first two kinds of outcomes.

Coherence is achieved not through detailed planning but as a natural consequence of the patterns of dialog employed and the relationships that might exist between outcomes. Integration is achieved not by top-down strategy deployment but through participation. Progress is made not through a linear, step-by-step process in which the incorporation of real-world learning likely comes at such a cost that it is resisted, but through an emergent process (Mintzberg, 1994) in which strategy development and its pursuit go hand in hand.

Below are the seven chapters in more detail:

PART I. INQUIRY

Chapter One. Context

Chapter One takes us to the beginning of a first workshop, the first opportunity for inquiry in a group setting. We will examine why context-setting is essential, deconstruct my favorite context-capturing (and often context-creating) exercise, and consider alternatives.

Chapter Two. The IdOO ("I do") Pattern: Ideal, Obstacles, Outcomes

Chapter Two introduces a conversational pattern central to this book, demonstrating it through a string of conversations held by a breakout group participating in a larger event. We then explore the pattern by abstracting from the details of their inquiry and the tools employed.

Chapter Three. Repertoire: Foundations for Setting the Stage

In Chapter Three, we look at a selection of reference models as sources of a rich repertoire of tools for inquiry conversations, including some already employed in the previous chapter. What do they teach? What does facility with these tools and their underlying frameworks look like? How do they translate into a participatory setting?

PART 2. MANAGING THE INQUIRY PROCESS AND ORGANISING ITS OUTPUTS

The following two chapters are about managing the inquiry process and organizing its outputs, both activities done to benefit the generative part to follow. As hosts, how do we establish direction? Where is convergence appropriate, and as hosts, what freedom do we have to calibrate it? How do we condense and consolidate the wealth of ideas generated into something manageable without losing the energy and commitment generated during inquiry?

Chapter Four. Calibration and Configuration

Chapter Four looks both back and forward. Looking back over the exercises introduced so far, what opportunities does the host have to set things off in the right direction with the aid of carefully calibrated *generative images*, *challenge questions*, and the like? Looking forward to agreement on the kinds of outcomes that will inspire action, how free or constrained will conversations need to be, and what kind of range is possible? Together, these perspectives help hosts structure events that will be relevant, engaging, and productive.

Chapter Five. Organizing for Generative Action

Is it coherent? Does it add up to something worthwhile? Chapter Five introduces different ways to organize the outputs of inquiry to avoid throwing valuable ideas away prematurely.

PART 3. GENERATIVE PROCESSES

The final two chapters take us into generative conversations, defined throughout the BMI Series as conversations that produce new ideas people want to act on. We'll look at the action that results from those and the not-insignificant challenge of sustaining the process.

Chapter Six. Ideation and Experimentation

Having up to this point focused on identifying outcomes that are widely understood and shared, in Chapter Six we actively solicit solution ideas through generative conversations. Our structure for this, *Meaning, Measure, Method*, is a derivative of Chapter 2's IdOO pattern. Then, to keep the experimentation process honest and to maximize the potential for future learning, we look at hypotheses big and small, experiments, probes, and measures of success.

Chapter Seven. Keeping Learning Alive

Chapter Seven is about ensuring that this generative experience isn't wasted. How can we ensure that the changes are producing the desired outcomes? How can we fail quickly, adapt and adjust as needed, and scale up those patterns of organizing that work best? Another pattern, *Right to Left*, will aid us. Working backward from key moments of impact and learning provides a perspective that helps the organization create *containers* for learning, each with the space to invite interesting things to happen and the focus to ensure the opportunity isn't squandered.

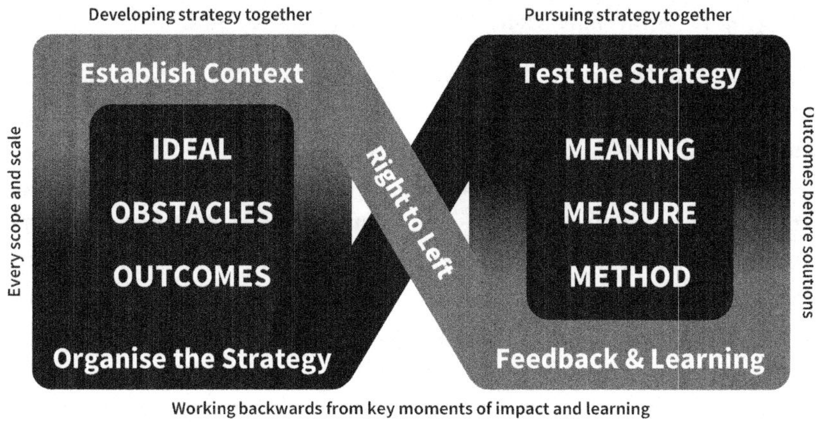

Figure 1. Three interdependent patterns: Ideal, Obstacles, Outcomes; Meaning, Measure, Method; and Right to Left

The activities and patterns introduced here sequentially are interdependent (Figure 1). We conduct inquiries into what's possible, anticipating future progress and learning. Organizing thoughts informs both inquiry and experimentation. As we put ideas into action, progress is measured less in terms of solutions implemented and much more in terms of the outcomes they do or don't bring about and what that means for the approach taken. At multiple scopes and scales—the importance of which we'll explore in the final chapter—we are developing and pursuing strategies together, each activity informing the other. Outcomes inspire action, validate solutions, and make us wonder what else might be possible.

Let me offer a metaphor if these chapters seem skewed toward inquiry at the expense of generative conversations. If the job of inquiry is to produce the catalyst for generativity, let's ensure we give that catalyst enough surface area that enough participants feel invited to engage productively. Moreover, if the overall process is to be self-sustaining—for which a necessary condition is that it creates more ideas than it consumes—its interdependencies must be considered. No part of the process can survive long in isolation.

Outcome-orientation

What holds the models and processes in this book together could be described as a core principle; I like to express it more generatively as a question, our big "*What if…*" question:

What if we put agreement on outcomes before solutions?

And to drive the point home: *authentic agreement on meaningful outcomes.* Authentic agreement requires the right people in the room—highly, if not maximally, representative of those who will need to do something different from what they currently do—agreeing on things that matter to them and expressing them in their own words. Meaningful outcomes mean not just numbers and targets but needs met, happy endings to stories, and the world changed for people in meaningful ways. And meaningful outcomes that are plural, plentiful, fractal, and part of a rich, diverse, and evolving landscape. This is a similar argument to that made by Bushe (2020) that a common purpose (outcomes), not vision (solutions), is needed to bring stakeholders into generative conversations and support emergent change processes.

These outcomes can be the raw material for strategy—a highly testable strategy that energizes transformation. Many of those outcomes will lead the way to solutions—perhaps multiple solutions—emerging at the right time from the people closest to the problem, people already motivated to find them.

This is *outcome-orientation*. I mean that term quite literally: when we're outcome-oriented, our direction is set by the outcomes we choose to pursue. Progress is measured in those exact terms, not by solutions implemented, problems solved, tasks executed, or plans followed. Not that those things are unimportant, but by taking an outcome-oriented stance, you are resolving not to be unduly distracted by them. Compared to the change-by-rollout approach I rebelled against all those years ago, outcome-orientation represents a 180-degree turnaround—a different paradigm entirely. Instead of using outcomes to sell monolithic solutions (Agile process frameworks, say), we use outcomes to find solutions, typically at a much more granular level. It's not just game-changing; it's an entirely different game.

Relation to other books in the BMI series

I've already mentioned one book from this series: Gervase Bushe's *The Dynamics of Generative Change* (2020), a short but essential reference for ideas foundational to this book, particularly the Generative Change Model.

There are three other books in the series that I would specifically like to mention. The first is Mark McKergow's *Hosting Generative Change: Creating Containers for Creativity and Commitment* (2020). *Hosting* gives us the metaphor of the host, which in the context of generative change gives a picture of a change process and a culture of welcome, participation, and belonging. Moreover, it leads us away from the idea of the facilitator as a coach, at their most potent when involved in each conversation, and towards the idea of the facilitator as host, responsible for creating and maintaining an environment where others can have some truly great conversations.

The other two are Tova Averbuch's *Initiating and Inviting Generative Change: Entry and Contracting for Emergent Outcomes in Results-Driven Organizations* (2021) and Sarah Lewis's *Creating Energized Commitment to the Dialogic Approach* (2024). Chapter 1 of this book starts with our first workshop, but much must have happened before. I am glad these two books cover those preceding activities better than I could. Here, we shall assume that the following are already in place:

- An engaged sponsor
- A 'planning team' or similar—people to help with event planning, to manage internal things like logistics and invitations, and to help set up follow-on activities
- Willing participants
- The right kind of challenge—probably not very well-defined (this is almost a given for reasons I'll explain in a moment), but sufficiently important to enough people for it to be motivating and energizing, and for which non-generative approaches are considered unsuitable or perhaps have failed already.

That "right kind of challenge" is the *adaptive challenge* referenced in the Generative Change Model. We're talking about the kind of challenge that isn't reliably tractable to *diagnostic* (as opposed to *dialogic*) methods. Because so much of the challenge will remain hidden until it is actively engaged with, relying on up-front analysis and prescription invites failure. Most cultural challenges fall into this category, as do many that involve significant external pressures.

Is there a "wrong kind of challenge"? If the challenge is essential enough—don't forget that this is one of our criteria—you probably won't regret having the organization enter into some kind of conversation about it, even in cases where a more linear approach could work. It is most inappropriate when it's inauthentic, where leaders go through the motions of a participatory and co-creative approach but where the result is largely predetermined. Selling solutions is not what this is about; attempts to do so won't pass unnoticed.

Relation to my previous books

Most recent first:

- The second edition of *Agendashift: Outcome-oriented Change and Continuous Transformation* (2021) covers similar ground to this book. More than twice as long, it's an exercise-by-exercise guide to the Agendashift workshops, with descriptions of the key tools and background on my sources. It emphasizes organization design and leadership more than I have space for here.
- *Right to Left: The Digital Leader's Guide to Lean and Agile* (2019, audiobook 2020) describes the Lean-Agile space in a deliberately outcome-oriented way. Both separately and together, in Lean and Agile, I still find plenty to celebrate; the frustrations I have alluded to in this introduction are relegated mainly to the footnotes.
- *Kanban from the Inside* (2014): My most significant contribution to the Kanban Method—and by extension, the Lean-Agile space—was an abstraction of that framework's principles and practices into a model of nine values. The model led to my first book, which remains a key reference in that space. There is a deep relationship between values and outcomes, and with the benefit of hindsight, I can see the seeds of something outcome-oriented and generative in that first book.

PART ONE

Inquiry

ONE

Context

At the start of a Dialogic change process, context is everything. Without context, rarely (if ever) does a business problem fully make sense. And once it makes sense, the real issue has often been misidentified.

Just imagine for a moment that there are gaps in understanding between workshop participants on any of the following points:

- The organizational scope of the exercise
- The range of business activities that are up for discussion
- Who (if not only themselves) each participant is expected to represent, and on what terms
- The underlying motivation for the event: is it business drivers, changes in external circumstances, etc.?

At one client, the motivation for an all-hands event was unclear beyond a vague sense that things couldn't continue as they were. More than once, I have been brought into organizations to help address localized issues of process and practice, only to find that a much more urgent challenge was to be found elsewhere, in a relationship with another part of the business, for example (one such example is described later in the chapter). Happily, I never needed to give the client the difficult news that the "presenting problem" was not what I should be focusing on—it emerged quickly and with a sense of shared ownership.

Now, imagine that those gaps in understanding go unacknowledged and unaddressed. Put yourself in those participants' shoes, and you understand how confusing or inhibiting the experience might feel. I learned this the hard way. Notwithstanding a few caveats we'll come to in Chapter 4, it seemed that every time I thought I might get away with not establishing context, I came to regret it later. Dealing with that unnecessary discomfort took time and energy I could ill afford to waste.

So, what is context? Informally, it's everything participants need to know to make sense of the conversations they're about to have. For those conversations to be productive, they need to know certain things in common. Context is shared and lives at the intersection of scope and situation.

"Everything" is a big word, and it might suggest that the way to start is with an extensive analysis. Unfortunately, the limited sharing involved in such exercises typically happens only between those who do the analysis and those who commissioned it. So, instead of analysis, think of context as the answer to this question:

Who and what are we dealing with?

For a manager or a coach needing to catch up on an ongoing situation for other colleagues, that's not such a bad question to ask. As the opening gambit for a workshop, though, it seems just a bit too open-ended, too detached from whatever purpose brought people there.

What does a participatory exercise need to do to capture context? One possible starting point is the following checklist, not so different perhaps from one a consultant might have in their head when visiting a client for the first time:

- **Identity:** How to identify the part of the organization (if not the whole) that we're concerned with
- **Mission:** What that part of the organization seeks to achieve; what it does, why it does it, who it serves
- **Scope:** Anything that helps to narrow the scope—specific activities, products, customers, constraints, etc
- **Challenges:**
  - Challenges that confront the in-scope part of the organization from the outside
  - Challenges that it sets itself from the inside
  - Challenges that aren't yet fully recognized, perhaps only beginning to emerge

Figure 2 provides a visual of this simple four-point list. I've found it surprisingly helpful:

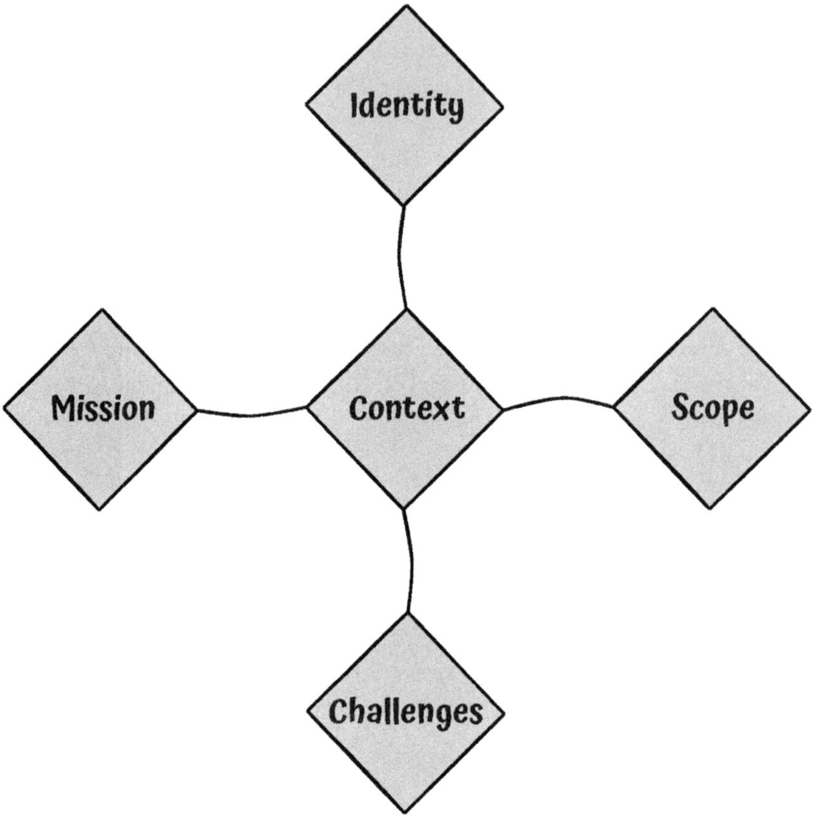

Figure 2. Establishing Context

At the top is **Identity**. That's the right place for it: much more than just a convenient label, it trumps all the others. If you ever get the response, "That's just not who we are," you are witnessing the power of identity.

On the left, **Mission**. Generative change is often about some combination of the following:

- Clarifying mission
- Adjusting it with small or not-so-small changes in direction
- Improving the capability to deliver it
- Enhancing the experience of carrying it out

Any or all of these may be open to challenge, but any attempt to change the balance between them and outside expectations will likely be deemed irrelevant or a distraction. Similarly, it's important not to overdo something in which participants already feel secure.

On the right, **scope** refers to those aspects of the organization that are part of the issue. It may be helpful to make the context smaller and less ambiguous by identifying the aspects of the organization most relevant to its key challenges. These might include process, structure, customer type, product line, or technology. Note that if they are the responsibility of a smaller part of the organization, it may be necessary to revisit Identity.

At the bottom, **Challenges**—in the plural and of different kinds to ensure we don't miss the important one. Challenges often have interesting interactions with mission and scope that can be worth exploring. Pay special attention if they appear to impinge on identity—a challenge to "who we are" or the group's continued existence. Identity crises don't happen often, but they can take an uncomfortably long time to resolve, so don't be too surprised if you find yourself invited into the middle of one.

You could turn my checklist into a participatory exercise, but it seems a dull way to begin a workshop! Let's try something more indirect and energizing.

Celebration-5W

Celebration-5W is my trusty context-capturing kickoff exercise. It can create some shared context even where little exists—at the beginning of a public training workshop, for example, where participants come from various organizations and backgrounds.

Although Celebration-5W works well as a whole-room exercise, I prefer to establish breakout groups from the beginning. It works well in person and online; henceforth, I'll use 'breakouts' to cover both table groups and online breakout rooms. For this exercise and all later exercises, you can assume the following structure unless mentioned otherwise:

1. A whole-room introduction explaining the premise of the exercise, positioning it relative to the overall flow, and explaining how it works
2. Where necessary, a demonstration or some whole-room practice, the host taking care though not to exert undue influence on the content of the conversations that will follow

3. Small group work, each breakout furnished with its own set of materials to work with
4. A whole-room debrief that focuses first on the experience of the exercise before bringing different contributions together as required

For this exercise specifically, here's the setup:

Imagine… You're celebrating!

- Celebrating your next big breakthrough
- Celebrating with everyone who helped make it happen
- Reminding each other how you were stretched and why it was all worth it

It can be helpful to provide an example of a celebration of this kind that you've attended yourself, a little of its context, the kinds of conversations you had there, how you felt, and so on.

After that whole-room setup, the bulk of the exercise occurs in breakouts where they will answer five questions. They must first agree on the What and the When, iterating between them until they settle on a meaningful level of challenge for a timeframe measured in months. Then, the remaining three: Who, Where, and Why. The task for the groups is to put that celebration into context with the (journalistic) 5W questions—Who, What, When, Where, and Why:

- **Who** is celebrating with you? (Your colleagues; others involved or supporting; perhaps your customers)
- **What** are you celebrating? (Your next big breakthrough and all that it makes possible)
- **When** are you celebrating? (The timeframe required for this significant and business-relevant challenge to be recognized)
- **Where** are you celebrating? (A venue that makes a statement about how this work is valued)
- **Why** is this important? (Distilled essence of *Why* for the whole endeavor—not just the celebration)

I like to encourage them to have some fun with the Where part and offer examples both from real life and past runs of the exercise, for example:

- The time I took my team to the cake shop across the road from my office in Budapest to celebrate a mistake that I—the CTO—had made
- The group that rejected my suggestion that they should party on a survey ship; although the proposal was relevant to their business and to me it sounded exciting, they couldn't wait to move out of their aging and unsuitable building and celebrate in the shiny new facility they could see going up outside

Like most exercises from the Agendashift stable, Celebration-5W is Creative Commons (CC-BY-SA) materials available at agendashift.com/resources. If you use the template designed by my friend Mike Haber (see Figure 3), ask them to start with the two boxes on the right-hand side of the page, iterating between them as necessary, then spiraling anti-clockwise toward the Why from there.

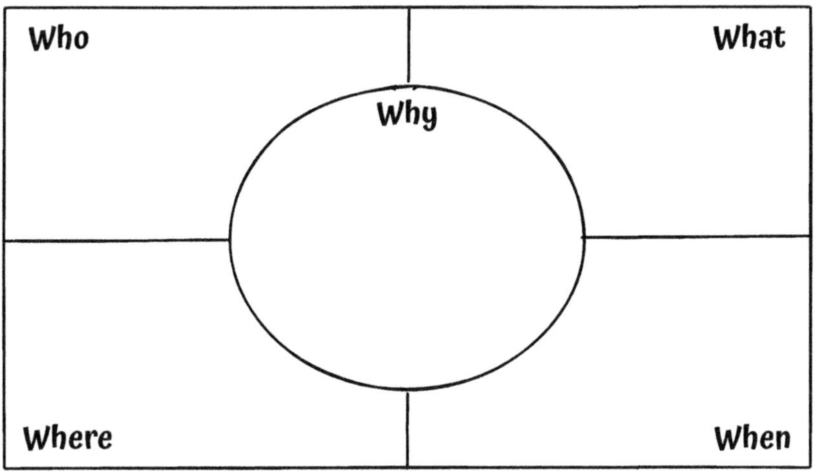

Figure 3. Celebration-5W template

During the whole-room debrief, I do not find it necessary to produce a combined artifact. We'll explore this further in Chapter 4, but for me—and this is representative of my approach to debriefs generally—it's enough that each breakout is aware of the others' work, informing future conversations. Some kind of group insight may be reached, but I don't force it.

Let's see how Celebration-5W fares against the four points for context from Figure 2. The first three points map straightforwardly enough:

- **Identity:** The Who covers this well, with the Where adding some color.
- **Mission:** That's addressed to a helpful degree by the Why, perhaps in conjunction with the What.
- **Scope:** The Who, the What, and the When all bring some clarity, likely the Why also.

That leaves the final point: **Challenges.** Although it may be hinted at in other elements of Celebration-5W, the element most closely related to the challenge is the "next big breakthrough" that's the cause for the celebration. This is introduced as part of the premise of the exercise and addressed explicitly in the What.

To go from breakthrough to challenge (in the singular now as we home in on the important one), ask this question:

- What's the overall challenge that makes your big breakthrough important?

Now might be the time to introduce the concept of the *adaptive challenge* if you haven't done so already:

- What's the adaptive challenge that makes your big breakthrough important?

For one mobile technology company I worked with, everyone wanted their new device to sell well, but that was months away. Kicking off with Celebration-5W, breakouts identified two entirely different challenges, both for similar timeframes, the end of the next quarter, four months away. One was technical: how to achieve volume production of something that existed only in prototype form so far. The other focused on sales: can we secure advance orders before establishing volume production? Only with some creative collaboration between the technology and sales teams, that's for sure! Both challenges were significant, and it was fitting that both were aired, but this second one would dominate the following conversations. The first one remained a key challenge for a smaller group, but they recognized that their contribution would also be critical to the second one.

On multiple occasions, I've seen breakout groups come up with product ideas and corporate strategy ideas that they have gone on to run with for the remainder of the event. Unless it's obvious that this will be a distraction from the real challenge in hand—and that's rare in my experience—I'm happy to follow their energy. Nevertheless, I have learned to pay attention to the coherence (or lack thereof) of what the different breakouts produce. Creative excitement is one thing, but a wide range of outputs with little resonance between them can indicate an organization struggling for direction.

If there seems to be little agreement on breakthroughs and challenges, another question worth asking:

- What is the purpose that makes these challenges meaningful?

This question is open enough that it's as likely to take the conversation toward organizational purpose as it is to the *"possibility-focussed purpose statement"* of the Generative Change Model. Either way, though, it is some shared context that is the basis for further conversation.

Alternatives to Celebration-5W

Celebration-5W belongs to a popular genre, the time travel exercise. Of those, there are a couple of valuable subgenres, one that looks forward to an idealized future and another that looks ahead to something more dystopian. A good example of the idealized future subgenre is Luke Hohmann's *Remember the Future* exercise, one of several product-related activities collected under the branding of *Innovation Games* (Hohmann, 2006). In that exercise, we send participants into the future—to a date that's some defined period ahead plus a bit more for good measure—asking them to solicit as much detail as possible on, for example, how the product in question is delighting its customers.

Remember, the Future is easily adapted (be aware that some published variants have done it without changing the name). For example, "Let's remember our upcoming *sprint* (our next timeboxed iteration), looking back on the amazing results we achieved and the awesome time we had together." The goal of that variant is to remind ourselves of how we wish to work and avoid some of the mistakes of previous sprints.

Gary Klein's (2007) *pre-mortem* is an example of the dystopian subgenre, emphasizing the avoidance of mistakes. "With the benefit of foresight, let us 1) imagine what killed our project and 2) commit to not doing that!" In a somewhat similar vein but without the time travel element is the *TRIZ* exercise from *Liberating Structures* (McCandless & Lipmanowicz, 2014). This exercise asks participants to think of all the ways the organization could mess up the endeavor. Then, they are invited to consider how many of those things they are doing already.

Dave Snowden and Tony Quinlan's (2018) *The Future, Backwards* combines the idealized and dystopian perspectives in one exercise. It involves telling the story backward from two maximally contrasting future endpoints—one impossibly good, the other impossibly bad—identifying turning points and other critical events until the story reaches the present. It is a sensemaking exercise; its goal is not to reach a "*do this, don't do that*" kind of conclusion but to maximize the number of things and perspectives considered.

Be aware that the spread of difficulty across these exercises is quite large; I started here with the easiest and ended with the most demanding of hosts and participants alike. Nevertheless, they are all worth considering, as is the time travel genre in general, if you want to design your own. But if your goals include obtaining context, an adaptive challenge, and a possibility-focussed purpose statement, Celebration-5W has plenty to offer.

TWO

Setting the Stage: Shared Ideals, Obstacles, and Outcomes

In this chapter, we will follow the conversations of a breakout group, one of several participating in a dialogic event. Through a string of conversational exercises, they will identify outcomes—things that participants want, the hoped-for results of change.

You can help a group identify ideals, obstacles, or outcomes in many different ways. My stories will show one way of doing it but don't get caught thinking this is the only, or even the best way, to structure those inquiries. Different situations will call for different processes. My point is that these three lines of investigation (ideals, obstacles, outcomes) form a foundation for taking a group or organization from the presenting problem to generative action. What's essential is that you surface and validate the variety of ideals, obstacles, and outcomes that currently live in the spoken and unspoken narratives of the organization you are working with.

What transpires in this chapter will read very much like a series of coaching conversations, but what is remarkable about them is that none of the breakout group's members has been placed there in a coaching role. If you look carefully for it, the coaching "hat" will seem to move from person to person. Similarly, although the event has an overall host, no one is designated to play that role in the breakouts. One member may "scribe" some critical thoughts, but that service is voluntary.

What makes these exercises work is a clear and memorable structure, each part employing questions that invite curiosity, sometimes playfully. That structure is the IdOO ("I do") pattern:

1. **Ideal**—envisioning a compelling future
2. **Obstacles**—identifying what gets in the way of what we want
3. **Outcomes**—looking beyond those to what's better

Beyond being used in a workshop, the IdOO pattern also has everyday applications. We are not training here, but the potential rarely goes unnoticed, and the experience "rubbing off" onto the every day has positive implications for the sustainability of the change process. The more the host sees themself as having an enabling role, the more likely they will make explicit the possibility of this transfer.

Before we get to the conversations, one thing to notice is what's not there: the *diverge/converge* pattern (Figure 4) and the push it represents toward convergence typical of facilitated decision-making.

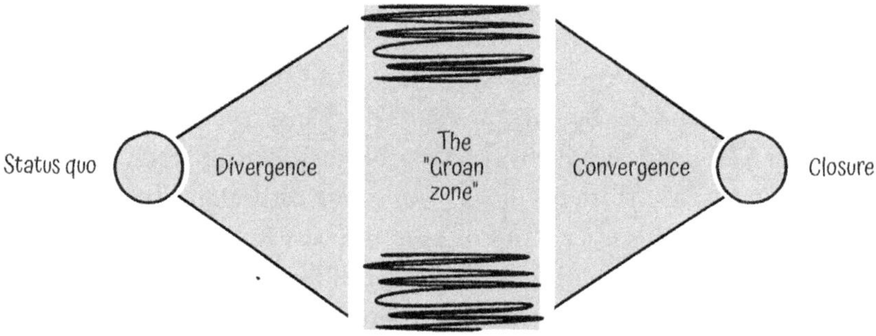

Figure 4. The Kaner (2014) model of group facilitation

The conversations we cover in this chapter may be constrained by time (breakouts starting and finishing together, for example), but that convergent push is otherwise absent. Instead, it's up to participants to decide which lines of inquiry they wish to pursue. They may leave some conversational threads dangling, perhaps to be picked up again later. Preceding conversations may have seeded others that seem to start from nowhere.

Transitions between distinct conversations (separate exercises, for example) can represent a change of direction and dimension. Multiple things and multiple kinds of things are generated during IdOO—obviously obstacles and outcomes, but also needs and stories. Stories feature explicitly in the Ideal conversation, and they may appear at any time subsequently.

Example conversation

We will follow the conversations of one breakout—group members Alex, Rowan, Chandra, and Jo—and also capture the gist of the whole room conversations between breakouts. Note that Nicky, the event's host, is present only for those whole-room conversations, introducing and debriefing each breakout exercise. It's worth repeating that none of the breakout groups have a designated host; Nicky has, however, provided handouts that participants can refer to.

Nicky's questions and other tools are not attributed in this chapter, but we'll spend some time with their sources in Chapter 3.

Ideal

With everyone together, Nicky introduces a reflection on the following words:

> Imagine…reaching the right customers, reaching their *strategic needs**, and achieving results in the way to which we aspire
>
> **strategic needs*: their needs, our strategy

Nicky: (repeating) Reaching the right customers, meeting their strategic needs, achieving results in the way to which we aspire.

For the moment, don't worry about what you don't yet have or that doesn't seem easy to obtain; just enjoy it!

What's that like when it's working at its ideal best for us?

What's that like when it's the best it could be? When it's the best it could conceivably be—let's stretch our imaginations here—what's that like?

And then the "what's happening" questions:

Whose needs would we be meeting?

What new stories could they tell?

In your breakouts, answer those questions as a group: What's that like, whose needs, what new stories? And enjoy it—enjoy it being the best it could be!

Reaching the right customers, meeting their strategic needs, and achieving results in the way we aspire.

In their first breakout:

Alex *"Reaching the right customers, meeting their strategic needs"*—I like that. It seems we know our customers pretty well, but I'm not sure that their needs and our strategy have yet come together in that ideal way. Something to work towards, I guess.

Rowan: Wouldn't it be great if we got ahead of our customers sometimes?

Chandra: So we're sharing what we're learning about them, learning to anticipate their needs, and before they know it, we're ready for them.

Rowan: Right. Although a part of me thinks this conversation needs to be directly about the customer, I don't feel that we're quite ready for that yet. For what you describe to be happening, we need to share more amongst ourselves.

Alex: Imagine looking forward to sharing something without someone else knocking you back with cries of "scope change!"

Chandra: So let's imagine it, coming to those meetings excited to share.

Jo: Expecting support and ideas rather than criticism.

Chandra: Loving it when it all comes together, and it wasn't an ordeal to get there.

Alex: Should we be writing this down?

Jo: I'm on it. How's this: Enjoying sharing what we're learning, adapting our strategies, innovating together, getting ahead of our customers, loving when it all comes together.

Rowan: Works for me!

Jo: We should do stories. Whose needs, what new stories?

Rowan: The customer thrilled that we got there before they did.

Chandra: *Us* thrilled that we got there before they did!

Jo: Let's not forget what you said about coming to the meeting excited to share. There's a little story right there and a happy ending to the struggle we're all experiencing right now.

Nicky brings everyone back together for a short whole-room debrief, beginning with the experience of the conversation so far and then its content.

Nicky: How was that? Where did it take you?

Rowan: Almost cathartic! I couldn't quite let go of what was bothering me about how things are for us right now, but at the same time, I imagined things being a lot better—and believed it too.

Chandra: I'm glad we're looking at recapturing a sense of enjoyment in our work. I hadn't made the connection with strategy before, and we haven't yet fully explored it, but I think there's something essential for us there.

In that first conversation, Jo served the breakout group by taking notes. That wasn't called for in Nicky's instructions; the goal was neither to analyze their situation nor to craft some response but to lift them out of the everyday and energize the following conversations. In that regard, Rowan and Chandra's feedback is quite typical. Nevertheless, some people find taking notes at this early stage helpful, and it is about to become more important.

Obstacles

While the preceding conversation remains fresh, Nicky introduces the next exercise in the same groups (they'll switch around in the next session). This takes the conversation in a new direction.

Nicky: Back to the here and now: What stops that? What gets in the way?

There is no need for theories or solutions, just what's in the way of all that you imagined—of it being the best it could possibly be, those needs met, those new stories.

Capture at least five obstacles—don't get stuck on just one thing—and don't overthink them. Keep it real, relevant, and representative: describe things your colleagues would quickly recognize that affect your everyday work, and word them as your colleagues might.

So, back to your breakouts! What stops that? What gets in the way?

Back in their breakout…

Jo: It's reassuring that the other breakouts came back with similar things. "Meeting each other's needs"—that hit the spot!

Alex: Meeting each other's strategic needs.

Jo: Exactly! Anyway… What stops that? All of that, I mean?

Chandra: I guess we don't understand our customers quite as well as we'd like. Maybe not even as much as we think we do.

Rowan: We just wait to be asked for stuff.

Alex: We wait to be told what to do, more like. And when we're not careful, they manage us (or at least try to), and I don't think that's right.

Rowan: But when we don't have much of a plan ourselves, can we blame them?

Chandra: Losing the initiative like that is perhaps what makes us so unhappy. And those meetings! Those awful meetings!

Jo: "Awful meetings"—got that. That's 7 or 8 now. Is unhappiness an obstacle or just a symptom? Both, I guess. I have the following obstacles now:

1. We don't understand our customers well enough
2. We wait to be asked
3. Our customers try to manage us
4. We don't have plans when we need them
5. We lose the initiative
6. We're unhappy

7. Awful meetings

And combining that first one with what that other breakout group said:

8. We don't understand each other's needs well enough

Alex: On reflection, I know it was me who said the one about customers trying to manage us, but really, I don't blame them. We resent it, obviously, but if we're honest, we leave them little choice, right?

Rowan: We leave it to our customers to manage us.

Jo: That's better, thanks.

Outcomes

It's time again for another quick turnaround. As before, Nicky holds a quick debrief (not shown here) that is just long enough for critical insights to be shared. Then, each breakout working off the obstacles they captured (plus any they might choose to borrow from others they've heard), the conversation takes another change of direction.

Nicky: And now outcomes! From obstacles to outcomes—one obstacle at a time, or all your obstacles together if that makes better sense:

Why is that important?—Take a moment to remind yourself why these obstacles are worth discussing.

What kind of…?—What kind of conflict, what kind of resolution, for example—plug in the word or phrase that needs clarification. This one's completely optional, but if your obstacle is in any way vague, this question is great for clarifying, and you can use it later with outcomes, too.

What would you like to have happen?—Take this as an invitation to turn the obstacle or obstacles into an outcome you want.

Then what happens? Then what happens? And again (and again): Then what happens?—from outcome to outcome, and yet more outcomes.

Here's a tip: Start small in answer to "What would you like to have happen?". Start with the first, tiniest signs that something interesting might be beginning to emerge—the most minor outcome you can think of, in other words. Then, go deeper into "outcomes space" as we call it. Those signs of emergence, then indicators of progress, measures of success—signs that we're winning, signs that we've won—and if you go deep enough, goals and aspirations. Starting small like that will give you more room for "Then what happens?".

And keep it meaningful: Needs met, happy endings to stories, the world changed for someone in some meaningful way.

Back in their breakout…

Chandra: Can we start with those awful meetings?

Alex: What kind of awful meetings? What kind of meetings? What kind of awful?

Chandra: Ha! I guess I asked for that! I want people to know that when they come to these meetings, they will get something out of it.

Jo: I suspect we aren't doing a great job identifying the shared goals that unite all our work.

Rowan: "Working towards shared goals" sounds like an outcome to me—certainly, I'd like to see more of it. And, like Chandra says, coming to those meetings with positive expectations.

Alex: Then what happens?

Chandra: Good question. Well, if those positive expectations are going to be met consistently, there must be people coming either with important things to share or with problems we can explore together—

Jo: (Interrupting) I make that two more outcomes by the way

Chandra: Anyway, that's better information sharing, and we're solving problems as a team. That makes for faster and better-informed progress, and then happier customers and happier teams in whichever order you prefer.

Alex: I wonder: will all of these conversations end in that same way, with "happier customers and happier teams"?

Chandra: Would it matter if it did? In any case, we could go further. With a better relationship between teams and their customer, the teams get more of the right kind of work. There's some kind of virtuous circle here, I'm sure!

Rowan: Going back a bit, if meetings are improving, perhaps more of that sharing and problem-solving will happen outside the meetings, too. Colleagues not saving up issues that would bc better dealt with right away, if you see what I mean. The "*Then what happens?*" is much the same but seems worth identifying separately.

The IdOO ("I do") pattern unwrapped

I describe the IdOO pattern—Ideal, Obstacles, Outcomes—as a pattern for strategy conversations, conversations that are about outlining or exploring "*a general plan to achieve one or more long-term or overall goals under conditions of uncertainty*."[1] As presented thus far, it falls short of that definition, but with that positioning, the significance of each part becomes evident if you consider skipping them.

What if you skip the Ideal part? If they're not challenged to think big, they'll likely default to thinking small. Their search space will be limited, they'll be dealing mainly with minor issues, and their results aren't likely to sell themselves.

What if you skip the Obstacles part? Now they have a strategy that isn't grounded in reality, severely—perhaps fatally—undermining its credibility and robustness. Who wants an approach that fails to meet relevant needs seriously and risks falling at the first hurdle it encounters?

What if you skip the Outcomes part? They risk getting seduced into solving problems that don't lead anywhere useful. They look prematurely for solutions of the wrong scale, whose implementation distracts from achieving business results.

The IdOO pattern is most easily understood as a sequence. Still, with practice, you learn to move easily between its parts, recognizing

1 en.wikipedia.org/wiki/Strategy

(for example) that coaching questions may be used to effect transitions between them (we'll see several of those in the next chapter). We can also center a new discussion on an outcome or obstacle identified in an IdOO conversation. That means the space we're exploring is fractal, with similar structures repeated at many scales. Practically, we can use the IdOO pattern to fill in gaps or dive deep into areas of particular concern. As we'll see in Chapter 6, that kind of inquiry can be an effective precursor to solution generation.

Ideal unwrapped

The Ideal part is often reflective, taking place mainly in breakouts. A key consideration is how you will focus ideation. How you frame the purpose of the inquiry can have a significant impact. Here is Nicky's typical introduction, reproduced in full to give a sense of its energy:

Nicky: Reaching the right customers, meeting their strategic needs, achieving results in the way to which we aspire.

For the moment, don't worry about what you don't yet have or that seems difficult to obtain; just enjoy it!

What's that like when it's working at its ideal best for us?

What's that like when it's the best it could be? When it's the best it could conceivably be—let's stretch our imaginations here—what's that like?

And then the "what's happening" questions:

Whose needs would we be meeting?

What new stories could they tell?

In your breakouts, answer those questions as a group: What's that like, whose needs, what new stories? And enjoy it—enjoy it being the best it could possibly be!

Reaching the right customers, meeting their strategic needs, achieving results in the way to which we aspire.

You want to focus people on the most critical outcomes. In the example, we saw Nicky begin and end with her preferred purpose: "Reaching the right customers...". That's the focus she is hosting.

When using the IdOO pattern, key issues for event design are a)the text of the focus, b)how it will be identified, c)or, if necessary, generated. More on this in chapter 4.

Next:

> For the moment, don't worry about what you don't yet have or that seems difficult to obtain; just enjoy it!
>
> What's that like when it's working at its ideal best for us?
>
> What's that like when it's the best it could be? When it's the best it could conceivably be—let's stretch our imaginations here—what's that like?

For the record, I will cite two influences. "*When you're working at your best, you're like what?*" is a question Caitlin Walker uses to invite work-related metaphors (see Walker, 2014). The idea that we can easily and continuously access a "compelling future" (my words) via an idealized version of the present I credit to Russell Ackoff (Ackoff, 1999).

And then the "what's happening" questions:

> Whose needs would we be meeting?
>
> What new stories could they tell?

About the stories part, another influence is the *job story* (Moesta & Engle, 2020), a way to bring to life a *job-to-be-done*. A single sentence will do; it just needs to capture two things authentically:

1. A 'struggling moment'—the when and where of a scenario in which a need arises.
2. The 'meaningful progress' made when that need was met, an outcome perhaps.

The first might be implicit. In a context dominated by unproductive meetings, for example, Chandra's "coming to the meeting excited to share" works just fine; someone's need was unexpectedly and wonderfully met, and the job done.

Obstacles unwrapped

How you ask for obstacles can significantly impact the quality of obstacles generated, with repercussions for later conversations. For a while, I used this gently curious question:

Q. What obstacle might be in the way of that?

More often than I would like, I found that this question would generate speculative answers that didn't land with other participants well enough to spark a productive conversation. After several iterations, I settled on this punchier wording:

Q. What stops that? What gets in the way?

Asked quickly (as one question, the first question mark effectively a comma), this deliberately unsophisticated question tends to invite many unsophisticated obstacles. The less sophisticated the obstacle, the less the risk of it hiding something potentially harmful to a productive conversation. Aware of that risk, Nicky gently introduces some constraints:

> No need for theories or solutions, just what's in the way of all that you imagined—of it being the best it could possibly be, those needs met, those new stories.
>
> Capture at least five obstacles—don't get stuck on just one thing—and don't overthink them. Keep it real, relevant, and representative: describe things your colleagues would quickly recognize that affect your everyday work and word them as your colleagues might.

Other approaches are possible. Chapter 4 describes a two-stage approach: an unconstrained "*What stops that? What gets in the way?*" followed by a step of review and revision.

The energy of the example breakout conversation is typical. People encounter obstacles all the time. Many, if not most, also have their own theories and solutions. We're tapping into that vital resource but framing the conversation so that empathy and agreement also come into play. As demonstrated by Alex, that empathy can extend beyond those in the room:

Alex: On reflection, I know it was me who said the one about customers trying to manage us, but really, I don't blame them. We resent it, obviously, but if we're honest, we leave them little choice, right?

Outcomes unwrapped

We'll take Nicky's introduction in parts. The first part connects back to the preceding exercise:

Nicky: Why is that important?—Take a moment to remind yourself why these obstacles are worth discussing.

What kind of…?—What kind of conflict, what kind of resolution, for example—plug in the word or phrase that needs clarification. This one's completely optional, but if your obstacle is in any way vague, this question is great for clarifying, and you can use it later with outcomes, too.

These questions can be used on things other than obstacles, and we'll see them again in the next chapter.

Then, from obstacles to outcomes, a definite transition:

Nicky: What would you like to have happen?—take this as an invitation to turn the obstacle or obstacles into something you want, an outcome.

Some participants may recognize the interestingly-worded "*What would you like to have happen?*" as a coaching question (covered in the next chapter); Nicky clarifies that this question invites an outcome. "*Then what happens?*" needs no explanation; what's important with this one is the rhythm:

Nicky: Then what happens? Then what happens? And again (and again): Then what happens? Then what happens?—from outcome to outcome, and yet more outcomes.

Reinforcing the expectation of progress that is set by that rhythm, Nicky uses a metaphor, "outcomes space":

Nicky: Here's a tip: Start small in answer to "What would you like to have happen?". Start with the first, tiniest signs that something interesting might be beginning to emerge—the most minor outcome you can think of, in other words. Then, go deeper into "outcomes space" as we call it. Those signs of emergence, then indicators of progress, measures of success—signs that we're winning, signs that we've won—and, if you go deep enough, goals and aspirations. Starting small like that will give you more room for "Then what happens?".

And finally:

Nicky: But keep it meaningful: Needs met, happy endings to stories, the world changed for someone in some meaningful way.

If *"measures of success"* might trigger unhelpful conversations about numerical metrics and target-setting, that last part can be adjusted:

> But keep it meaningful! Not "5% more, 10% less", but "needs met, happy endings to stories, the world changed for someone in some meaningful way."

That isn't to suggest that numerical metrics can't ever be useful, but they must be kept in their place. The issue might be avoided with a different language choice, but I'm glad to get it out in the open. I want *outcome* to be associated with meaningfulness.

The debriefs

Nicky treats the three exercises, Ideal, Obstacles, and Outcomes, as one extended conversation punctuated by opportunities for each participant to briefly organize their thoughts, look objectively at what just happened, and prepare for the following discussion. There are as many conversations as there are breakout groups, plus one more, the whole-room conversation. Content-wise, it's a matter for each group how much cross-fertilization occurs. If groups diverge, more ground is covered. Where they converge, an important theme has likely been identified.

As we'll see in the following two chapters, the Obstacles and Outcomes conversations can be more involved than shown here, and their respective debriefs will be covered there. There is also the issue of how to organize what has been generated, especially significant numbers of outcomes. Sitting between inquiry and generative conversations, that pivotal activity gets a whole chapter: chapter 5, Organizing for Generative Action.

The IdOO pattern, wrapped

With practice, the IdOO pattern can be used as a quick routine, taking only moments. In Chapter 6, we'll see it embedded in another pattern, reconnecting with and expanding on a single outcome before generating multiple (and diverse) solution ideas. As part of the agenda for a session of strategic inquiry, however, I typically bracket it as follows:

1. **Establish context**—Who and what are we dealing with?
2. The main conversation:
   - **Ideal**—Envisioning a compelling future
   - **Obstacles**—Identifying what gets in the way of what we want
   - **Outcomes**—Looking beyond those to what's better
3. **Organize the Strategy**—What's our Agenda for Change?

The context part was addressed in Chapter 1. The Organize the Strategy part is the topic of chapter 5. The *Agenda for Change* is an Agendashift term; it begins (chapter 5) as a *theory of change*, a set of relationships between outcomes, hypotheses about what might lead to what, from which focuses for attention, and measures of progress and success are readily identified. Later, there are solution options (Chapter 6), some chosen to test or implement. Taken together with the obstacles and a suitable purpose statement, the Agenda for Change is a strategy. Combined with a process that encourages solution ideas to be generated and tested over time, thereby feeding back on the strategy (Chapter 7), it becomes the focus and expression of something emergent.

THREE

Repertoire: Foundations for Setting the Stage

In the form of questions, Chapter 2 introduced tools you may have recognized for surfacing shared ideals, obstacles, and outcomes. They're drawn from a rich repertoire of three well-established sources: Challenge Mapping (Parnes & Basadur, see Basadur, 2003), Solutions Focus (Jackson & McKergow, 2011), and Clean Language (David Grove, whose ideas are available from several authors mentioned below). We will try to understand something of their intent, how they work in the hands of a specialist, and what more the generalist practitioner of generative change might learn from them.

Your existing repertoire may include tools you prefer to those I mention. My goal in this chapter isn't to sell you my personal favorites (even if they are that) but to demonstrate how a range of tools can be adapted for self-facilitation and outcome-orientation, resulting in the kinds of conversations we saw in the previous chapter. By 'self-facilitation,' I mean that the tools can be used powerfully by groups of people with no designated facilitator, increasing the likelihood of transfer into day-to-day work life. By 'outcome-orientation,' I mean that we attach much greater importance to outcomes than solutions in developing and pursuing strategy. Outcomes provide direction, and they beget solutions, the latter held lightly until tested against results.

It's important to respect the context in which each model was developed, the purpose to which they were initially (and still are) applied, and their underlying theory. Taking tools from one context to another without adjustment often ends badly, and I'll be transparent about any changes I have chosen to make. Let me stress that no criticism of the source models is implied. On the contrary, if you feel my changes say more about me than they do about the models, that's entirely fair! That said, I believe the IdOO pattern does provide a way to appreciate and integrate these different tools, even where the fit seems less than perfect.

Challenge Mapping

Challenge Mapping has enjoyed a recent resurgence thanks to the Design Sprint (Banfield *et al.*, 2015), a community dedicated to helping product organizations generate and test product ideas rapidly. However, it is decades old and traceable back to the 1960s, particularly the work of two pioneers of applied creativity, Sid Parnes and Min Basadur.

As the name implies, Challenge Mapping has a visual aspect (see Figure 5), but we'll look first at a dialogue between two characters from Chapter 2, the host Nicky and participant Chandra. In the following snippet, "unproductive meetings" has just been established as the focal challenge. This example shows how a facilitator would use Challenge Mapping to frame a conversation to identify where new ideas are needed.

Nicky: Chandra, let's explore one of the obstacles raised in this morning's breakout. Which one would you choose?

Chandra: Let's go with those awful meetings.

Nicky: Why that one?

Chandra: I'd like people to know that when they come to these meetings, they will get something meaningful out of it. That's not happening often enough right now.

Nicky: What stops that?

Chandra: There are too many updates that just aren't that relevant. It is more about what's keeping people busy instead of what we need to work on together.

Nicky: What stops people from giving more relevant updates?

Chandra: A couple of things: I suspect we aren't doing a great job of identifying goals that would give the meetings more focus, but there's also a safety issue. Too many people feel that they have to justify themselves every day.

Nicky: That second one first: Why is that important?

Chandra: People won't be giving their best if they're always looking over their shoulders.

Nicky: And the first one? Why is identifying goals important?

Chandra: Well, people's work will be better aligned with clearer goals. And we'd have more meaningful ways to measure progress.

Nicky: What stops you from having that?

Chandra: Actually, not much! They're there, or at least I think they are, but not at a level we would want to reference daily. Perhaps that's why we're here!

There are two kinds of questions here:

1. 'Why' questions that take the conversation 'up' in the direction of meaning and motivation
2. 'What' questions take the conversation 'down' in the direction of concrete detail

The 'Why' questions here in the example:

- Why that one?
- Why is that important?
- Why is identifying goals important?

Here, they are all intended to elicit things like rationale and significance. Ask enough of the right kinds of 'Why' questions with the right tone and timing, and you get to the heart of the issue.

Explicitly or implicitly, the 'What' questions are all in on the theme of "What stops that?" generating what would be called 'challenges':

- What stops that?
- What stops people from giving more relevant updates?
- What stops you from having that?

As Figure 5 demonstrates, a Challenge Mapping conversation is "scribed" in a particular way. Each response is re-framed as a *"How might we…?"* (HMW) question. For example, if the group says the way to improve daily meetings is to make them more meaningful, we turn that into a question and write, "*HMW make our daily meetings more meaningful?*".

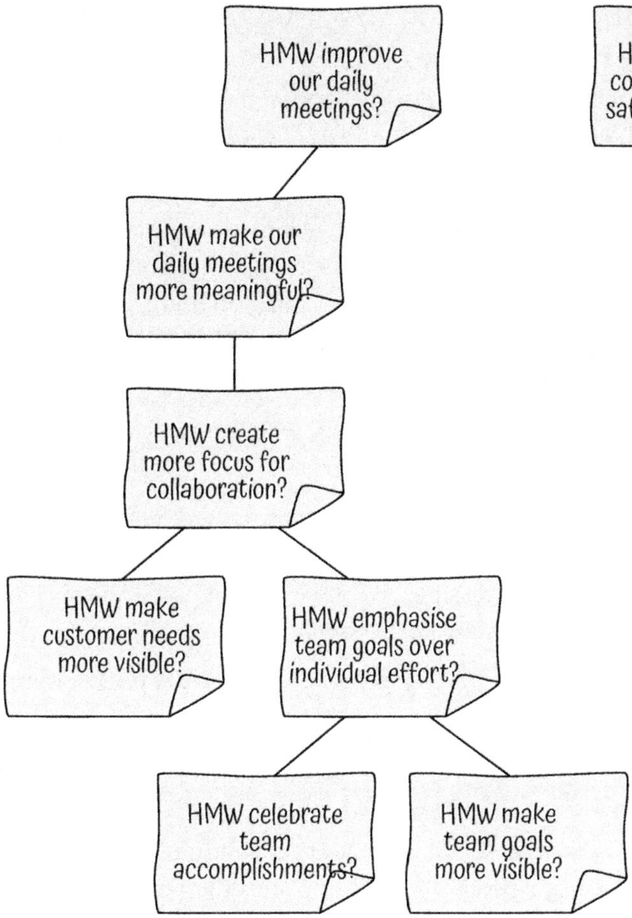

Figure 5.A Challenge Map

The spacial placement of an HMW sticky is up or down (for 'Why' or 'What' respectively) relative to the one about which its question was asked. That tends to place the most abstract HMWs at the top of the map ("HMW improve our daily meetings?", for example) and their corresponding detail ("HMW make customer needs more visible?" and "HMW celebrate team accomplishments?", for example) below. The finished map does three things:

1. It communicates some shared understanding of what challenges related to what other challenges, and by extension, where there might be leverage

2. It facilitates decision-making conversations about which challenges to focus on
3. Its language explicitly invites the generation of creative solutions for a focal challenge either directly or through one of its descendants

Conventionally, a facilitator leads a Challenge Mapping exercise, often with the help of an assistant who captures answers on sticky notes in the "*How might we?*" (HMW) form. A lot is going on there, more than I am generally brave enough to expect breakouts to achieve unsupported. Still, Challenge Mapping leaves its imprint in several ways:

- *What stops that?* (followed immediately by *What gets in the way?*) to solicit obstacles in the IdOO pattern
- *Why is that important?* As a focusing question. Recall Nicky's commentary: "Take a moment to remind yourself why these obstacles are worth discussing." We'll see another application of *why that is important* in the next chapter.
- *How might we?* As a prompt for generating ideas that people want to act on (Chapter 6)

Solutions Focus

Solutions Focus (Jackson & McKergow, 2011) is Solution-Focused Brief Therapy translated from psychotherapy into non-therapeutic settings, particularly coaching. It operates under the following premise: even where clients seem 'stuck,' they can find solutions—small solutions at their fingertips and perhaps beginning to work already—but need help to see them. Get unstuck for long enough for the solution process to be repeated a few times, and perhaps some potentially life-changing idea will emerge.

Let's see this approach taken with Chandra's issue of poor meetings:

Nicky: On a scale of 1 to 10, where 1 is the worst meeting you have ever experienced, and 10 is the best, what number best describes these meetings?

Chandra: Oh… [Pause] Well, it has to be less than 5—I sometimes wonder if they're doing more harm than good. 4 on a good day, more often a 3?

Nicky: That's interesting. What do you think separates the 4 days from the 3's?

Chandra: Well, for me personally, the more people there are involved in the topics I'm most interested in, the better the meeting will be.

Nicky: Now, suppose that some miracle removes everything that prevents tomorrow's meeting from being a 10. And it's a 10 for everyone! What's different?

Chandra: Oh wow. Ok. The main thing is that it's clear that everyone wants to be there. That means either they've got something exciting to share, or they know that they're about to get involved in something really interesting, or both.

Nicky: Great. You didn't know that this miracle happened. You went to the meeting expecting a 3, and it's a 10. What's the first thing you notice telling you that something unusual might be happening?

Chandra: People sharing and stuff?

Nicky: Before that, the first clue?

Chandra: Ah, I see what you mean. I guess it's how people are when they arrive. What might have preceded that, I don't yet know of course. Intriguing!

That snippet illustrates two techniques from Solutions Focus:

1. *Scaling*, measuring something onto a numerical scale as a way to turn something experienced into something observed
2. The *miracle question,* a future-focused question that invites consideration of what it might be like to have a situation's problems removed

Underlying both techniques is the assumption that there are always solutions to be found. In the case of scaling, the measured experience is never quite the same twice. Between those varying experiences, perhaps a "difference that makes the difference" (Bateson, 1972) is waiting to be uncovered. If direct experience provides insufficient variation for this approach, imagine slight variations in the score and work on that instead. Chandra, for example, scored those meetings 3 or 4. What separates 4 from 3? What might a 5 look like?

At first, the miracle question seems to be about thinking big, but again it's about those slight differences, the initial, tiniest clues that something good is happening—a sign that things are getting better or that the opportunity for that may have been seeded. Thinking small in a big space, unstuck, and with something to aim for.

I am not a therapist and can't speak to Solutions Focus's application in therapeutic settings. I'm not even trained as a Solutions Focus coach. What fascinates me is how it translates into group settings. No pun intended, but it scales up brilliantly:

- Everyone's experience is different (even their experience of the same situations), massively increasing the range of variations considered
- The chances that one participant's problem might find its match in another's solution are again massively increased

We'll see the scaling technique applied in the next chapter. Meanwhile, some of the spirit of miracle question imbues the IdOO pattern's Ideal, and there is the explicit recommendation to start with small outcomes, those "first, tiniest signs that something interesting might be emerging" before other leading (and still inconclusive) indicators of progress. Small isn't nothing. Small is unstuck!

Clean Language

Clean Language's premise is simple: by keeping conversations uncontaminated by the practitioner's assumptions, the client can develop and explore their own understanding and *model*. In a highly disciplined form of curiosity that treats the client's point of view with exquisite care and respect, the hope is that helpful insight may be reached.

Like Solutions Focus, Clean Language has translated successfully from psychotherapy to individual and group coaching and has much to teach the facilitator and host. Its originator was a UK-based New Zealander, the late David Grove. A growing community continues his work, and I recommend books by Sullivan & Rees (2008), Walker (2014), and Way (2013).

Practitioners employ a repertoire of Clean or 'cleanish' questions in a Clean conversation. 'Cleanish' refers to questions (stock or invented at the moment) whose cleanliness—their freedom from assumptions—may be contextual. Forty or so questions are regarded as canonical. Most of these questions include placeholders for other words or phrases to be inserted; they're for the client's own words, verbatim.

Clean Language's most characteristic question is the one used to invite metaphor:

Q. *Those* unproductive meetings, *they're like what?*

Whatever those unproductive meetings are like, the metaphor is the client's, not something the practitioner suggests.

I should confess that I don't use this question often. However, I embrace Clean Language's curious, assumption-free questioning discipline and use eight other Clean questions to model (metaphor alert!)—a 'landscape' of obstacles and outcomes. I present these eight questions on a cue card (Figure 6), and introduce them as a self-facilitated game for small groups called 15-minute FOTO (From Obstacles To Outcomes in 15 minutes). For this book, to make it easier to see how the card is used, I've labeled questions A – H in the order they appear in the text below.

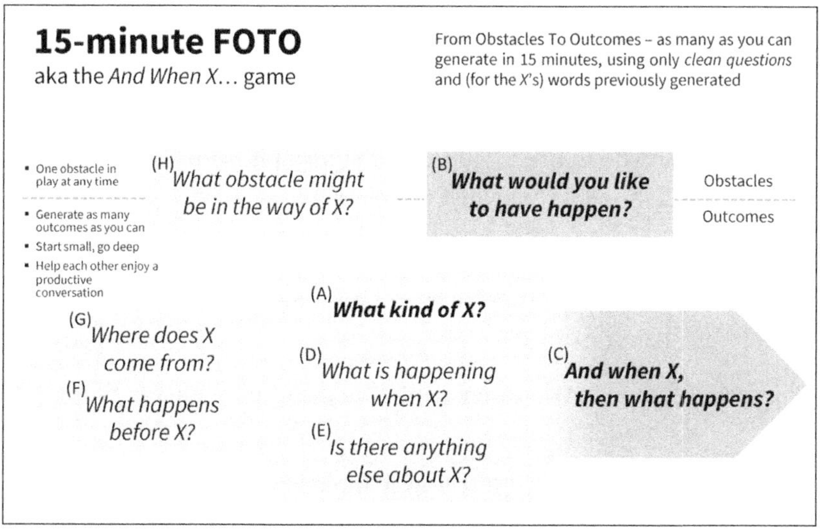

Figure 6. 15-minute FOTO cue card

The game comes in 'Lite' and 'Classic' formats. The Lite format—recommended for first-time use—involves a breakout discussion in which anyone can ask a question, and anyone can answer, including answering one's own question. In the Classic format, participants rotate for a few minutes at a time through the roles of client, coach, and host—an altogether more intense experience that may be best saved until you can use the game a second time with that group. In both formats, the game's objective is to capture as many outcomes as possible, subject to the constraint that each outcome must answer a question from the card, in which any inserted words accurately recall something previously generated.

Of those eight questions, the first three (A, B, and C in the figure) are by far the most heavily used and highlighted in bold. Slightly unrealistically then, here is Nicky demonstrating the use of all eight questions, Chandra having raised once again the now-familiar topic of unproductive meetings. Replacing the X placeholders, insertions are shown in single quotation marks, and I've labeled each question from A to H so that you can find them more easily on the cue card (Figure 6 above).

Nicky: What kind of 'unproductive meetings'? (A)

Chandra: You know the kind—people just showing how busy they are.

Nicky: And when 'people just showing how busy they are,' what would you like to have happen? (B)

Chandra: I'd like them to genuinely look for opportunities to collaborate.

Nicky: And when they 'genuinely look for opportunities to collaborate,' then what happens? (C)

Chandra: We'll see them teeing up follow-up conversations.

Nicky: What's happening when 'looking for opportunities to collaborate'? (D)

Chandra: It's obvious that they will value the opportunity to work with others

Nicky: Is there anything else about 'looking for opportunities to collaborate'? (E)

Chandra: Honestly, I wish most people were collaborating with others most of the time

Nicky: What happens before 'looking for opportunities to collaborate'? (F)

Chandra: People arrive properly prepared, knowing what issues they want to share, and with a desire to collaborate on them

Nicky: Where does that 'desire to collaborate' come from? (G)

Chandra: Good question. A problem shared is a problem halved?

Nicky: What obstacle might be in the way of that 'desire'? (H)

It's possible to play the game with just the first three questions, and I will expand on those a little.

"*What kind of…?*" (A) is a more open alternative to "*Can you be more specific?*", one I now prefer in everyday conversation. In the game it works on both obstacles and outcomes, generating more specific versions of the obstacle or outcome in question. The more concrete the obstacle, the easier the subsequent conversation (more on that in chapter 4). Later, if we get so deep into 'outcomes space' that things begin to feel distant, it can be used to draw the conversation back into more familiar territory.

In the previous chapter, we saw Alex use this question playfully:

Alex: What kind of awful meetings? What kind of meetings? What kind of awful?

There was perhaps a missed opportunity:

Alex: I wonder: will all of these conversations end in that same way, with "happier customers and happier teams"?

Someone might have asked:

> What kind of happier customers? What kind of happier teams?

As we saw in chapter 2, "*What would you like to have happen?*" (B) generates outcomes from obstacles. I recommend introducing it as Nicky did:

Nicky: *What would you like to have happen?*—take this as an invitation to turn the obstacle or obstacles into something you want, an outcome.

…

> Here's a tip: Start small in answer to "What would you like to have happen?". Start with the first, tiniest signs that something interesting might be beginning to emerge—the most minor outcome you can think of, in other words. Then, go deeper into "outcomes space" as we call it. Those signs of emergence, then indicators of progress, measures of success—signs that we're winning, signs that we've won—and if you go deep enough, goals and aspirations. Starting small like that will give you more room for "Then what happens?".

With or without its *"And when…"* prefix, *"Then what happens?"* (C) does most of the work of the inquiry. Given an outcome, it will almost certainly generate another one. If asked repeatedly, a whole series of outcomes can be generated. As an observer, I notice that the inexperienced coach often worries on the client's behalf about the repetition long before the client does and bails out. That's a shame because these deeper forays into outcomes space often trigger the most profound insights.

Here's that same demonstration again but focussing now on the generated outcomes, which I've numbered:

Nicky: What kind of 'unproductive meetings'? (A)

Chandra: You know the kind—people just showing how busy they are.

Nicky: And when 'people just showing how busy they are,' what would you like to have happen? (B)

Chandra: I'd like them to be genuinely looking for opportunities to collaborate. (1)

Nicky: What kind of 'opportunities'? (B)

Chandra: Solving problems together. (2)

Nicky: And when 'solving problems together,' then what happens? (C)

Chandra: Their work gets unblocked (3) and we make faster progress. (4)

Nicky: What kind of 'unblocked'?

Chandra: Well, perhaps they found a novel solution (5), or one of them knew who to ask (6). Could be anything!

Nicky: And when 'we make faster progress,' then what happens? (C)

Chandra: We're happier (7), and our customer is happier too (8).

Nicky: And when 'we're happier and our customer is happier,' then what happens? (C)

I make that eight outcomes from the first six questions. Not bad!

Some questions are more likely than others to yield solution ideas, these most of all:

Nicky: What's happening when 'solving problems together'? (D)

Chandra: After the main meeting, small groups get together to work on a specific problem.

Nicky: What happens before 'small groups get together'? (F)

Chandra: Issues are raised in the meeting, and when we catch ourselves getting into a level of detail that's irrelevant to the majority of participants, we arrange an impromptu meeting.

Nicky: Where does that 'impromptu' come from? (G)

Chandra: We need to develop habits of resolving issues quickly, not holding onto them until the next scheduled meeting.

The goal of the game is to generate outcomes. No harm done, however! Given a solution idea, "*Then what happens?*" can be expected to create an outcome.

The 15-minute FOTO debrief begins with the experience of the game:

- When you're the client, answering those questions, what's that like?
- When you're the coach, asking those questions, what's that like?
- What's that like when you're the host, seeing what's happening, scribing the outcomes, and helping others have an enjoyable and productive time?

It might seem illogical to start with the client, but it's so encouraging if you do! Any worries that coaches may have had about how they were coming across to their clients are put into their proper perspective and mostly disappear.

That worry dealt with by the debrief naturally turns to the most challenging aspect of the inquiry, the discipline of keeping one's assumptions under control and resisting the powerful urges to diagnose problems or suggest remedies before the client's model has been explored. That's what's challenging about the coaching role, but that's the point. If the experience and the subsequent reflection rub off, the inquiry is worth a good deal more than just its outputs.

An informal but thoughtful sharing of key talking points and insights generated during the inquiry follows. Focusing mainly on outcomes, organizing the captured outputs is a separate exercise (Chapter 5).

Start small

The materials for 15-minute FOTO (available via agendashift.com/resources/15-minute-foto) include this tip:

- Start small, bullet-point answers

That's shorthand for something I like to practice as a whole room before breakouts and done with something of a Solutions Focus flavor. We can imagine Nicky doing this:

Nicky: We will practice starting small, using "*What would you like to have happen?*" as an invitation for a small outcome. *What would you like to have happen?* What first, tiniest signs of progress might we see? Could someone shout out their most concrete obstacle? Your most specific, least ambiguous, least abstract, most concrete obstacle?

Nicky: Before that, even tinier?

Nicky: And after those first, tiniest signs, how will we know we're moving in the right direction? *And when …, then what happens?*

Nicky: (Several times) *And when …, then what happens?*

Next, there's a second round of practice on their "most abstract" obstacle, modeling the use of "*What kind of…?*". For example:

Nicky: What kind of 'unproductive meetings'? (A)

Chandra: You know the kind—people just showing how busy they are.

Immediately, the conversation is focused on something much more specific. Continuing:

Nicky: And when 'people just showing how busy they are,' what would you like to have happen? (B) Again, start small, those tiniest signs.

Chandra: I'd like them to be genuinely looking for opportunities to collaborate. (1)

Nicky: What kind of 'opportunities'? (B)

Chandra: Solving problems together. (2)

Concrete obstacles and small outcomes create more space for "*Then what happens…?*". In gameplay terms, they make the conversation easier and generate more outcomes (higher scores, if you like). There is a practical benefit, too: when the time comes to move from outcomes to solution ideas and action, those small outcomes often represent good places to start.

PART TWO

Managing the Inquiry Process and Organizing its Outputs

FOUR

Configuration, Calibration, and Framing

Chapters 1, 2, and 3 have introduced some structures and conversational tools for forms of inquiry designed to elicit ideals, obstacles, and outcomes. A collective inquiry into those three creates a container for future coherent, generative conversations. The previous chapters gave you my best thinking on how to have that inquiry, but it's not the method that matters; it's ensuring the people in the conversation get to say and hear what they want (ideals), what purpose they serve or wish to serve (outcomes) and what's getting in their way (obstacles). You might call this "getting everyone on the same page," but it's far more complex than that. No one knows exactly where this is going, and the flux, ambiguity, and novelty are part of it.

Chapters 6 and 7 will examine how we can use that container to catalyze generative conversations, action, and learning. But to get there, we first need to answer two questions. This chapter: to set up generative conversations, how should the initial inquiry be approached? Next chapter: How do we manage ambiguities sufficiently to focus and energize creative effort?

Informed by what in some circles is known as *complex facilitation*[2], which goes out of its way to avoid premature convergence, in this chapter we will:

1. As promised in Chapter 1, take one last look at context.
2. Consider different ways to inquire into ideals, obstacles, and outcomes.

2 cynefin.io/wiki/Complex_facilitation

3. Identify where convergence is most likely to happen in those inquiries and suggest ways the host might choose their words to avoid triggering it unintentionally.
4. Look at one part of the conversation (specifically, Obstacles) in which careful doses of prioritization or re-framing can be helpful.

To help motivate those last two points, it is not difficult to imagine inquiries converging on just one obstacle. That might not seem terrible, but I've seen change initiatives lose momentum because most participants see a singular obstacle as "someone else's problem"—perhaps something their sponsors should address on everyone else's behalf—hardly a recipe for generative change. Or, possibly worse, people get stuck on how hard the change process is presumed to be before the inquiry has even started. A method that expands on a broad front is much less vulnerable to these genuine issues, not to mention the increased opportunity for generative action it creates.

One last look at context

In Chapter 1, I described context 1) as everything participants need to know to make sense of the conversations they're about to have and 2) as living at the intersection of scope and situation.

There are tradeoffs to consider. For example, a narrower context (a quality problem in a particular business process) is easier to understand. To those for whom it is relevant, it is easier to engage with. The flip side, of course, is that a narrower context can exclude people, perhaps unhelpfully. Conversely, a broader context (employee motivation, for example) may engage more people but possibly at the cost of it being a more challenging bit of work.

Before choosing, designing, or introducing a context exercise, ask yourself these questions:

- Could it be that context is already well established by the organization's scope and the specifics of its situation as given or implied by the invitation or prework? (See later in this chapter about a critical kind of prework, the assessment).
- If we need to narrow or broaden context, which dimension needs the most adjustment: scope or situation?

Be careful that you don't prejudge the outcome by narrowing the organizational scope. Maybe the situation deserves broad and diverse representation. Perhaps the same issues impact different parts of the organization in very different ways, but the opportunity to explore them from various directions will still be helpful. Maybe the content of the inquiry is sufficiently independent of scale that it applies to every scope. When you think of how many different ways the same issue can show up in different organizations and how many adjustments to client circumstances are needed to make a dialogic intervention work, you understand why the editors of this series want books that go beneath recipes to talk about the chemistry of the ingredients.

If in doubt, err on the side of extending the invitation to more people rather than fewer and see who engages (see Mezick & Sheffield, 2018). You've learned something if the response is other than what you expected. If necessary, you can adjust the scope, offer, or both.

Beginning the inquiry

Recall these words from the introduction to the Ideal inquiry in Chapter 2:

> *Imagine…reaching the right customers, reaching their* strategic needs*, *achieving results in the way to which we aspire*
>
> *strategic needs: *their needs, our strategy*
>
> *What's that like when it's working at its ideal best for us?*
>
> *Whose needs would we be meeting?*
>
> *What new stories could they tell?*

The questions (or variations thereof) are common to most ideal inquiries. The opening words, however, were chosen for the event. Looking at them more closely, they split into two parts, each representing a different approach to strategy, *outside-in* and *inside-out*:

- "*Reaching the right customers, reaching their strategic needs*" begins the inquiry outside the organization—with its customers. If we take an outside-in approach, the conversation proceeds inwards from there, with the implications for organizational alignment explored with each step.

- *"Achieving results in the way we aspire"* is more about what's happening inside the organization—with its internal experience and capability. Although with *"results,"* the door remains open to considering the outside impact of the organization's work, the intention here is inside-out.

Both phrases have a generative quality to them. They are implicitly (and in the second one explicitly) aspirational—*possibility-focussed* and *purposeful* without in any way prescribing or constraining the content of the conversations that will follow. Being provided by the host as part of the event design, they are not precisely the possibility-focussed purpose statement of the Generative Change Model. However, there may be times when you want such statements to be created by the participants, not the sponsors. The more detailed discussions of the outside-in and inside-out strategy below include two ways to generate those.

Outside-in strategy

When designing an outside-in strategy conversation, the obvious challenges are how to start it and how then to move it in an inward direction. Both offer opportunities to generate a possibility-focused purpose statement from the participants.

One alternative to the *"Reaching the right customers"* text is to pose it (or one of your own) as a question:

- What is happening when we reach the right customers and meet their strategic needs?

With or without the aid of an Ideal-style reflection (of which the "Whose needs, what new stories" part seems particularly relevant), a possibility-focused purpose statement can be the expected output. Some real examples:

- "An effective presence in Asia" (for an ambitious design agency based in Europe)
- "The go-to place for meeting informational and training needs" (for a membership organization in the professional development space)

To establish an inward trajectory, you can ask for responses to that statement to consider the customer perspective first and the organization's perspective second, i.e., outside before inside.

Where do you take it next? I use a preset structure:

1. Customer
2. Organization—perhaps to address issues of positioning and identity
3. Product—the products and services through which those needs will be met
4. Platform—all the capabilities needed to support the preceding
5. Team(s)—what it means for everyone involved

You could use that structure or another or improvise on the day. Sequence the elements (or "layers") in outside-in order, and for each aspect, again consider outside and inside perspectives in that order. You will notice—and can emphasize—a process of alignment: each successive conversation considers needs identified earlier.

If you plan to use the IdOO pattern, note that you don't need to use it in full for every layer. For example, you might do Obstacles and Outcomes for multiple layers at a time, perhaps even just once. It is also possible to do Outcomes fewer times than Obstacles.

Inside-out strategy

When the approach to strategy begins with internal experience and capability, it can be helpful to work at different levels of detail. That suggests a different kind of sequence to plan for. For example, you might have two separate events to do the following:

1. To set the scene, and as a secondary objective, to familiarize participants with the process
2. To identify and work on more specific issues

Some practitioners like to reverse the order of those:

1. Work on familiar low-level issues but in new forms of inquiry
2. Step back to a more thoughtful consideration of key challenges, overall direction, and so on.

Which approach you take may depend on the nature of the engagement. Be aware that many practitioners, coaches especially, find the lower-level work well within their remit, but for the higher-level conversations, they struggle to get the invitees needed to make those conversations productive. Without senior leaders, it's hard to achieve more than localized improvements.

You'll need some way to start the higher-level conversation. *"Achieving results in the way we aspire"* might do, and again, you can frame it as a question. You may want something with a little more texture or designed to fit what you know of the context; the hard part is crafting something non-prescriptive. I sail a little close to the wind here with language quite close to Lean's *"just in time,"* but this text (see Burrows, 2017) has served me well for a long time:

> Imagine...
>
> Everyone able to work consistently at their ideal best:
>
> - Individuals, teams, between teams, across the organization and beyond
> - Right conversations, right people, best possible moment
> - Needs anticipated, met at just the right time

This is tailor-made for a great Ideal conversation, and I have witnessed some cathartic moments from this kind of inquiry. Even in the most well-meaning and purpose-driven organizations, people's everyday experiences can feel painfully different from what is carefully alluded to here. The opportunity to imagine a work environment free of its dysfunctions (whatever they may be) can come as enormous relief.

For lower-level conversations, an assessment is one way to get to the issues. The hard part is to design one that isn't prescriptive; participants don't respond well to being sold to! Mine use this style guide, which can also be used by participants in an exercise to create their own assessment prompts, either reflectively to close an event or to increase an assessment exercise's coverage:

- **Inclusive**—Start each sentence with "We" or "our" and make it a statement that you believe most of your colleagues could embrace
- **Present tense**—not impossibly out of reach; perhaps there are pockets of this happening already
- **Non-prescriptive**—avoid specifying practices or other means by which this outcome will be achieved; instead, allow multiple approaches

These all conform to the three criteria:

- We often work together in small groups, focussing our efforts and developing our knowledge and skills together
- We are trusted to make our own decisions
- We recognize how our customers' needs and behaviors have evolved over time

At some appropriate time after participants have completed their assessments (at the event or as prework), scoring each prompt, the host debriefs the consolidated survey. To avoid offering unsolicited and judgemental diagnoses, I find it helpful to focus less on strengths and weaknesses and more on areas of consensus and divergence. Especially in a diverse group, consensus may point to some pervasive constraint that might be changed through generative action. Divergence creates the opportunity for participants to tell contrasting stories. Good stories, which I invite first, may inspire action where things work less well.

Assessments also create opportunities to use *scaling* (recall Solutions Focus in Chapter 3). For example:

Host: This one's interesting: "*We meet regularly to review how we work and the results we're achieving.*" At least a quarter of the scores are 1's, and nearly that many are 4's—that's the whole range! Starting at the good end first, what experiences might explain the 3's and 4's we're seeing here?

Host: And the 1's and 2's? What experiences might explain those?

Host: How might we explain the differences? Some variation might legitimately be explained by differences in interpretation, organizational scope, recent experiences, awareness of what's possible, and so on, but could there be more to it than that?

Host: What's the slightest change that might tip someone over to give the next highest score? What might move someone from a 1 to a 2? From a 2 to a 3? 3 to 4?

The IdOO pattern works well when going from assessment prompts—typically not of the participants' own design—to outcomes that participants are motivated to act on. I use it with two straightforward modifications.

The first, which you can think of as completing the "Establish context" step that typically precedes the Ideal, Obstacles, and Outcomes steps, is for breakout groups to prioritize just the few assessment prompts (five, say) that best identify areas where further inquiry is most needed. The second modification is to the Ideal questions:

- Why is that important?
- What's that like when that's working at its ideal best for everyone?
- Whose needs would we be meeting? What new stories could they tell?

Given that each group is reflecting on choices they have made themselves, it does not seem presumptuous to begin with "*Why is that important?*". The question helps participants let go of the provided text and encourages them to express some of their motivations for choosing it.

Discussing obstacles

This apparently straightforward step is not without its pitfalls. What could be simpler?

- What stops that? What gets in the way?

Recall, however, Nicky's cautions:

> There is no need for theories or solutions, just what's in the way of all that you imagined—of it being the best it could possibly be, those needs met, those new stories.
>
> Capture at least five obstacles—don't get stuck on just one thing—and don't overthink them. Keep it *real, relevant, and representative*: describe things your colleagues would quickly recognize that affect your everyday work and worded as your colleagues might express them.

Ensuring a productive inquiry into obstacles

There may be no wrong answers when leading an inquiry into obstacles, but that doesn't mean that answers can't be improved! Some obstacles just aren't conducive to productive conversations, and with the help of a group in Berlin that got seriously stuck, we worked out why.

When you know what to look for, the most typical signs of unhelpful obstacles are easy to spot:

- **Tribal shorthand**—any language likely to include one group at the expense of others (any jargon, for example) or that points the finger (at managers, customers, or at a particular team, for example)
- **Scarcity language**—obstacles that start with "Lack of…", "Insufficient…", "Poor…" or similar—often attempting to sell a theory, diagnosis, or solution, and almost always expressible in a more productive way
- **Wishful thinking**—wishing for some unobtainable resource, or by some platitude wishing the whole challenge away (wishing for a better culture or a better mindset, for example)

Instead, what you want to ensure is that the group identifies obstacles that are *real, relevant, and representative*:

- **Real**—actually experienced as obstacles, not easily dismissible as theories, diagnoses, or solutions
- **Relevant**—having some material impact on the challenge in question
- **Representative**—described as those who experience it might explain it, and describe something they would choose to prioritize for attention

Where time is limited, it is possible simply to draw participants' attention to these issues and hope they will produce high-quality obstacles in a single exercise. However, the experience and the results of the exercise both improve significantly if you split the exercise into two parts. In the first part, breakouts take "*What stops that? What gets in the way?*" at face value, answering as quickly as they wish. Then, they look for and deal with the abovementioned signs in a much more considered review pass. That is not because we're the "language police"—far from it, we want participants to feel they can express themselves—but because the effort will pay off later.

As host, I like to give that reframing significant emphasis:

- Challenge yourselves and each other to eliminate any of these obstacles that others would find:

– Blaming or judging

– Selling solutions or theories

– Focuses on what isn't, not what is

– Avoiding concrete issues

Obstacles framed as "what isn't" show up as things like "Lack of people" (or money or time). Later discussions of these will, at best, lead to wishful thinking and, at worst, a sense of powerlessness. Changing the obstacle to something like "excessive workload" is more likely to generate imaginative solutions.

- Before moving to breakouts, it's helpful to explain the differences with past examples: "Lack of a knowledge management system" (this favorite example of selling a solution came from my very first workshop)
- "Lack of time" (or some other hard-to-obtain resource, the less interesting side of an imbalance)
- "Management" (or some other group)
- "Culture" (or something similarly hard to agree on)
- And my favorite:
- "Lack of the X mindset"—tribal shorthand, selling a solution or a theory (perhaps both), quickly received as judgemental, and telling the less interesting side of the story, not describing what people experience

Digging a second time into obstacles may be well worth it in longer events. Breakout groups often find it hilarious when they catch themselves repeating past mistakes; it all helps make learning much more powerful. There's a leadership lesson, too: any leader serious about improving the discourse of their organization might start with how they articulate obstacles. For that reason and others, be ready to give this exercise the debrief space it deserves.

From obstacles to outcomes

With a good list of obstacles and using this book's patterns, you have two main options as host. You might take the generative conversations route and get quickly to solutions (Chapter 6). Or, as assumed in this chapter, you keep following through on the IdOO pattern, aiming to organize outcomes into a representation of strategy (Chapter 5), presumably to generate solution ideas afterward. The tradeoff is straightforward: an organized strategy can be useful, and your sponsors may expect it, but it takes time to produce. Here, I will assume that continued inquiry will be time well spent and point out a few details that might otherwise be missed.

First, here is Nicky in the introduction to the Obstacles exercise:

> Capture at least five obstacles—don't get stuck on just one thing—and don't overthink them. Keep it *real, relevant, and representative*: describe things that your colleagues would quickly recognize that affect your everyday work and worded as your colleagues might word them.

It is perhaps a minor point, but if we're paying attention to how we avoid anything likely to induce convergence, the wording of "*at least five obstacles*" is quite carefully chosen. "*Five to ten*" (which I have used) is unnecessarily specific. On the other hand, "*several*" isn't quite specific enough—it's likely to raise further questions. I've found five to be a good number of obstacles, but too many are better than too few, and there's no need at this stage to distract from the exercise at hand by drawing too much attention to it.

The second relates to this invitation to "go deep" and two later comments:

Nicky: Here's a tip: Start small in answer to "What would you like to have happen?". Start with the first, tiniest signs that something interesting might be beginning to emerge—the most minor outcome you can think of, in other words. Then, go deeper into "outcomes space" as we call it. Those signs of emergence, then indicators of progress, measures of success—signs that we're winning, signs that we've won—and if you go deep enough, goals and aspirations. Starting small like that will give you more room for "Then what happens?".

...

Alex: I wonder: will all of these conversations end in that same way, with "happier customers and happier teams"?

Chandra: Would it matter if it did? In any case, we could go further. With a better relationship between teams and their customer, the teams get more of the right kind of work. There's some kind of virtuous circle here, I'm sure!

If the inquiry is taken far enough, generating increasingly distant and (typically) more abstract outcomes, it can only go to so many places. It should not be surprising if they get onto themes of customer satisfaction, team satisfaction, effectiveness and/or efficiency, business success, sustainability, and so on. Also, many of those thematic outcomes feed off each other; the longer conversations proceed, the higher the chance that they identify a virtuous circle.

Nicky's advice is calibrated about right. Not every conversation will get to aspirational outcomes (outcomes that will help both organize and motivate the strategy), but participants are at least primed for the possibility, and promising inquiries will be pursued for longer. She avoids undue bias by not mentioning specific outcomes (thematic or otherwise). And although she might mention virtuous circles, they are probably better left until the debrief. The more instructions and advice she gives, the more there is to remember, and a point will come where adding to it only makes it harder for everyone. If participants find the conversation going around in circles, they will deal with it at the time, and so can the debrief.

Taking stock

The different tools integrated in Chapters 2-4 each bring something of value, for example, care with assumptions, attention to scale, and a focus on what's important. Underpinning the structure of the IdOO pattern is a principled commitment to agreement on outcomes before solutions, the authenticity of which depends on invitation, representation, and participation on equal terms. As we shall see in Chapter 6, these interventions do not preclude generative conversations—i.e., conversations whose purpose is to generate solutions—but the process described thus far has been one of inquiry.

If you haven't done so already, now might be a good time to take stock yourself. When, as host or coach or in some other role (manager, perhaps), you operate in the realms of inquiry, what constitutes your personal repertoire? What is its dynamic, and by what mechanism—pattern or otherwise—is that dynamic produced? And by what principles, commitments, or other constraints is coherence assured?

FIVE

Clarifying and Organizing Outcomes Before Searching for Solutions

Suppose you were the host in the case described in Chapter 2. In that case, you might worry that the breakout group whose conversations we followed could be torn between mending a broken customer relationship and improving certain aspects of the internal experience, their meetings being a specific sore point. Moreover, their breakout was only one of several. What did they make of what other groups shared? When multiple groups do their own inquiry, doesn't that make things even more complicated?

Many facilitators would treat this as a problem that needs resolving. Through a facilitated decision-making process, options would be narrowed down, and priorities would be agreed upon. But from a Dialogic OD point of view, we are not trying to whittle things down; we are trying to help people expand their possibilities. As represented by outcomes, we want them to be plentiful and abundant.

By construction, the groups' outputs are related to each other. That means they can be organized—not to reduce choice, but to make it easier to see the range of options available and to help people make their own decisions about how they will act on them.

Even with just the two main issues of our example, several possibilities arise:

- The group indeed splits into two, one part to work on the customer relationship, the other to work on the internal experience
- The group decides to focus on one issue now and the other later

- The group decides to focus on only one issue, discarding the other
- The group decides to work on one issue in the hope or expectation that it will have a bearing on the other
- The group decides that the two issues need to be worked on together

Any of these options might be reasonable, even optimal, depending on circumstances. They are likely all preferable to doing nothing, and the fact that we have people motivated to do something is a big win! But those last two possibilities are intriguing. We have not just two issues, but in the shape of a relationship between them, a new idea. It might be no more robust than a hypothesis, but that's ok: hypotheses can be tested. In short, by organizing their ideas, additional focal points for action—new *affordances*—have been created.

Again, back to the group we followed in Chapter 2, some members will already be thinking about how to make the customers' needs more central to their process. Whether in connection with that challenge or separately, some will be engaged in the pressing need to raise morale and a potential quick win in the celebration of recent successes. Toward the other end of the ambiguity spectrum, some will be mulling over questions of safety. There is plenty to be getting on with!

Dealing with ambiguity

Before we get to the practicalities of organizing for generative change, spare a thought for a moment for the leaders involved. We will be organizing outcomes in the presence of significant ambiguity. Much of leadership consists in seeing and managing the actual and potential relationships between things—not just between outcomes as we will be dealing with here, but between people, between groups of people, between activities, and so on, and also between different kinds of things: person to group (and back), person to activity (ditto), group to activity, and so on. Part of the task of leadership is to reinforce through reiteration of agreed-on relationships. Nevertheless, leaders must recognize when it's time for relationships to be reconsidered and to see the possibility of new relationships, perhaps before anyone else does.

Ambiguity makes all of this harder, not only because the relationships are harder to see and more challenging to be sure about. The difficulty is more than technical; when leaders identify themselves with something uncertain, they invest some personal capital.

Fortunately, they don't need to carry that burden alone: with a participatory approach, many more people will be invested in ideas they have helped develop. And is there a viable alternative? By this stage, it should be apparent that a linear, designed-up-front change strategy would not be up to the task.

Different ways to organize

By design, inquiry processes tend to generate many ideas of one kind or another. That can present some practical difficulties:

1. The number and variety of items generated and captured
2. The range of possible interpretations of each item
3. The range of possible responses each interpretation invites

In terms of the *kinds* of items—challenges, obstacles, outcomes, etc.—generated thus far, I shall limit this chapter to looking only at outcomes. Even so, the above difficulties can multiply alarmingly.

We shall look at techniques to deal with difficulty 1 (number and variety) sufficiently to make difficulty 2 (ambiguity of interpretation) seem quite manageable. As we organize, our understanding changes, and ambiguity reduces.

What about difficulty 3, of which a large part is *solution ambiguity*, the range of solutions that the organization could be willing to contemplate? In a generative change process, we make a virtue of it! You may remember this line from the introduction: "*Solutions emerging from the people closest to the problem, people already motivated to find them.*" It's a well-rehearsed line (I credit my friend and collaborator Karl Scotland for the first part of it), and you could say that by choosing both here and previously not to deal in solutions, we demonstrate our confidence in that generative process. But making a virtue of solution ambiguity doesn't mean we're ignoring it; implicitly and later explicitly in this chapter, we manage it.

In a generative change process, like that described by Bushe (2020), you may not need to do any of what follows in this chapter—you want people to choose the ideas they want to work on and launch as many experiments as possible; what their ideas mean will emerge as people work on them. The generative change strategy is a 'try stuff out and learn as you go' strategy.

Sometimes, however, that won't work; instead, you use a 'high-engagement' strategy (Bushe & Lewis, 2023). High engagement can be appropriate whenever any of the following apply:

- The group has to make choices—perhaps because significant capital outlays will be needed or interdependencies among solutions mean you can't just try stuff and learn as you go.
- Proposals have to be made to people who are not present. For whatever reason, people can't make decisions during the meeting. As Lewis (2024) emphasizes, you really want to avoid this if possible because it will drastically slow down the change process. However, sometimes you can't.

Sometimes, even if you are aiming toward a generative strategy, you may believe:

- Participants will find value in taking stock of all the ideas they have produced, a desire perhaps to see how their diverse contributions fit together
- There will be a need to evaluate future progress in the light of these conversations (we shall see in the next chapter that this can be valuable)

What follows is for those conditions. The techniques described in this chapter are highly visual, all well suited to sticky notes on a whiteboard, but many are workable in other media. They are:

- With some strong reservations, the ever-popular duo of Affinity Clustering and Dot Voting
- Organizing outcomes into columns—Plan on a Page
- Two exercises that make full use of the available space, the Cynefin Four Points Contextualisation Exercise and Option Relationship Mapping

Affinity Clustering and Dot Voting

Together, these techniques narrow down a large and diverse set of ideas to a manageable few, hopefully creating shared meaning. In a change process, there are a couple of places where I might be tempted to use it:

1. Near the beginning of the process, when prioritizing challenges or obstacles.
2. Much later in the process, if we must select from a range of solution ideas.

These two techniques are easy to facilitate—hence their popularity—and often go together. As one combined exercise and with some possible variations, it works as follows:

- Write the ideas that need organizing onto separate sticky notes
- Participants bring their stickies to the board, placing them more or less thoughtfully; you may invite participants to describe their items to the group as they do so
- Related stickies are grouped and named in a self-organized way or done by the facilitator in conversation with the whole room. The "affinity clustering" part of the exercise reduces the number of items by clustering similar ideas and giving them one label.
- With the permission of their originators, you can combine groups of very similar stickies to avoid splitting the vote.
- People vote for items they want to take forward for further discussion by placing dots next to the clusters. You can purchase sheets of sticky dots at most stationary stores or by 'dotting' them with marker pens.
- Participants can have more than one vote (3 is typical) to spread or concentrate as they wish for that last step.

I begin with this technique only because it is so popular. I rarely use it outside certain meeting formats, mainly those that start with an empty agenda, like OpenSpace and Lean Coffee. Its downside is that items that don't get enough votes are quickly forgotten. When used later in a meeting, it can be the visual equivalent of agreeing only to next steps and throwing the meat of the preceding conversation away. What a waste! If you're only going to come away with next steps, call it a next steps meeting!

Plan on a Page—strategy as a theory of change

Several formats can be described as a "Plan on a Page." I'll explain a simple one that effectively organizes the outcomes generated by a single breakout group for presentation. Outcomes are organized under three headings, Short Term, Medium Term, and Long Term, with those terms being relative to each other—i.e., they need no calibration by the host.

These instructions are sufficient to yield at least an initial organization:

- In the **Long Term** (rightmost) column first, place your most aspirational outcomes, those best able to serve as goals overall
- In the **Short Term** (leftmost) column second, place your most actionable outcomes
- Between those, in the **Medium Term** column, place those intermediate outcomes that tell you that you are winning, making real progress towards those goals and aspirations.

The most ambiguous outcomes will typically be found towards the right and the least ambiguous towards the left.

Secondly, we organize by ambiguity explicitly but vertically:

- Beginning again with the Long Term column, sort outcomes vertically such that your most ambiguous outcomes—those most open to the broadest range of interpretation and solution options—come last, at the bottom; then resequence them as you wish so that as you read down this column, it reads from least to most ambiguous.
- Working backward—Medium Term and then Short Term—arrange outcomes vertically to make their relationships with outcomes in the column to their right most apparent

As shown in Figure 7, these relationships are made visible. Here, if outcome A points to outcome B, this expresses a belief that A supports, takes us in the direction of, helps to bring about, will inform our thinking (etc.) about B. The reverse relationship also carries meaning; the belief B in some way depends on, benefits from, is preceded by (etc.) A.

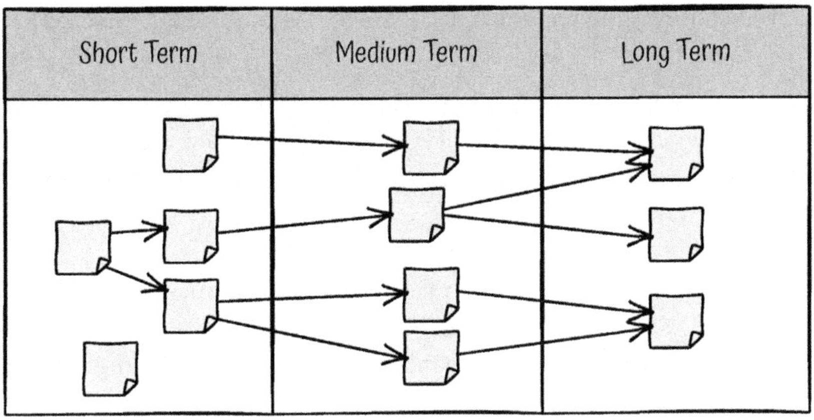

Figure 7. Plan on a Page with relationships

I should stress that when engaging with an adaptive challenge, these relationships can only be hypotheses about tendencies. Nevertheless, they're helpful for two reasons:

1. By relating A and B, we're choosing to consider B from the direction of A and vice versa, and our understanding of both, therefore, changes
2. Hypotheses can be tested; by identifying the relationships, we further increase our change strategy's surface area, each relationship representing another affordance

The Cynefin Four Points Contextualisation Exercise

I have already described a number of techniques for organizing outcomes:

- Clustering by relatedness of content
- Organizing under predefined headings (with care, the Plan on a Page's headings can be replaced, perhaps with something more model-driven)
- Sorting by ambiguity—done here for the sake of presentation (i.e., to tell a stronger story), but a practical technique in its own right as it makes adjacent items easier to compare, which is helpful when prioritizing, for example

- Hypothesizing relationships of antecedence, subsequence, and impact

Not to defer action but to prime participants for it, these techniques enable outcomes to be viewed from different directions, helping people find new meaning in them and thereby make decisions about where and how they want to act despite the significant ambiguities involved. This is organizing as *meaning-making*.

In that vein, If you are familiar with the Cynefin framework (Snowden & Boone, 2007), Dave Snowden's Cynefin Four Points Contextualisation Exercise can be used to organize granular inputs of various kinds: problems, symptoms, or stories, for example. It works very well with outcomes, and it helps them be approached in the right way. It scales better than Plan on a Page and (as described below) can be used to integrate the work of multiple breakouts.

Rather than explaining it all up front, it works better to reveal the steps one at a time, and the underlying framework comes last, revealed in the created visualization. The host's job is to pace the exercise carefully, sustaining an atmosphere of thoughtfulness and openness to insight. Deliberately adding a layer of intrigue, I keep the exercise's official name secret until after it has finished; I introduce it under what is explicitly a pseudonym, literally as "Option Approach Mapping (not its real name)." To the connoisseur of visualization techniques, what's interesting about this exercise is its use of space, which it needs plenty of.

Ask participants to write all their outcomes separately on sticky notes. You will begin by defining the space as follows:

Slowly complete each step before introducing the next:

- Looking at all your outcomes, choose "*the single strongest example of one where there's an approach to accomplishing that outcome we can all see and agree on*"; place that one in the bottom right corner (each breakout might each place their best example tightly in the corner so as not to obscure any others).

- Now, for the top right corner, choose "*the single strongest example of one where an expert or some research will determine a good approach*"—an approach you can confidently follow.

- Continuing anticlockwise, top left: "*there's no one right approach—experts will disagree*"—10 experts will give you ten different ideas.

- And bottom left: *"no known approach is immediately apparent"*—beyond urgent symptomatic fixes and trying to work out what's going on, all bets are off; we don't know where to start

Especially if you are integrating multiple breakouts' work, getting this far may already have taken several minutes. We continue slowly:

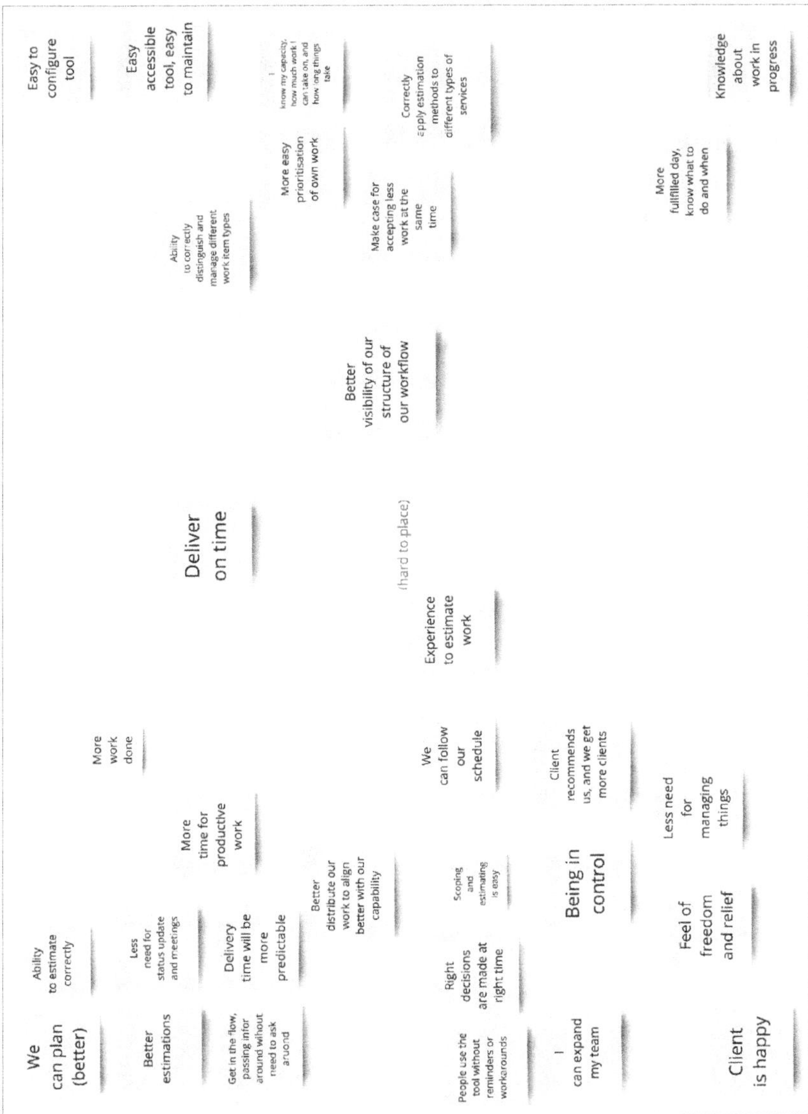

Figure 8: Example of Completed Option Approach Map

- Now, choose one outcome at random (one sticky per breakout, not one per person). Thinking carefully about how those first four items were placed, to which of the corners is it drawn? In terms of approach, does it belong near one of them, somewhere between two of them, or is it pulled three or four ways? Place it best you can, and if you really can't do that authentically, place it right in the middle
- And your next outcome, relative to the five already there, again in terms of approach
- And the next
- And the rest, one at a time (at this point, I discourage participants from grabbing multiple stickies at once)

Once all of the stickies are placed, you'll see something like Figure 8.

As host, it's now your turn. As thick as you can make them, and deliberately passing through any stickies that might seem to lie on some invisible border, draw four boundaries that each take in each of the four corners and together take in all but any of those otherwise unplaceable centrally-placed stickies (see Figure 9).

For participants who have realized what is happening, this is a moment of vindication. I've asked everyone not to spoil the surprise, but now's the time to introduce the Cynefin framework (Snowden & Boone, 2007) and its five *domains* of *clear*, *complicated*, *complex*, *chaos*, and *disorder*—respectively, the regions around the corners that took those first four stickies and that central region for the otherwise unplaceable stickies.

The slow placement of stickies isn't merely about categorizing each outcome but contemplating them in relation to others. If we had started with headings or internal borders, the experience would have been vastly different. Even mentioning the name 'Cynefin' changes the experience for anyone who has heard of it, hence my use of the pseudonym.

The careful avoidance of quick categorization in this exercise models the deliberate avoidance of some real-life category errors that can be wasteful, expensive, or worse. For example:

- Taking a linear approach (*complicated*) to the kind of outcome that needs to be approached emergently (*complex*), or vice versa
- Making hard work of something everyone can easily agree

on (*clear*) or rushing to a quick fix in a situation where understanding is limited (*chaos*)

- Identifying it as one kind of thing when really it is several (*disorder*) and in need of breaking down somehow

Be aware that in this exercise, where outcomes are placed depends on both context and understanding, neither of which are fixed. Run this

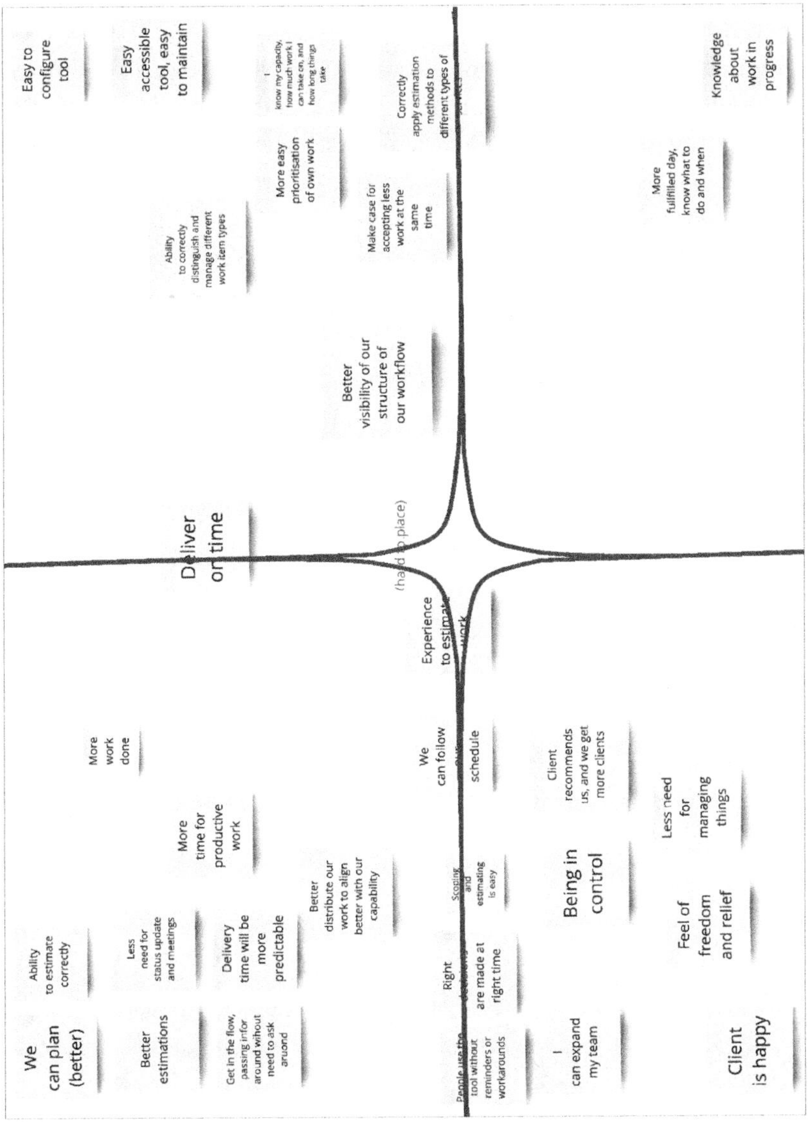

Figure 9: With Cynefin Boundaries Drawn

exercise at another time, and the same outcomes might be positioned quite differently.

Option Relationship Mapping

Using the four corners, the Cynefin Four Points Contextualisation exercise (aka Option Approach Mapping) makes good use of space. Option Relationship Mapping, the final mapping tool of this chapter, also spreads outcomes across the whole space, with reference, this time not to its corners but to its sides.

Option Relationship Mapping was conceived of by my friends Liz Keogh and Karl Scotland as an outcomes-friendly mashup of Wardley Mapping (Wardley, 2018) and Cynefin (such that if you're keen enough on these exercises to do both Cynefin Four Points and Option Relationship Mapping in sequence, step 1 below becomes noticeably easier).

Unlike the Four Points exercise, giving an overview first is helpful.

1. As illustrated in Figure 10, with a relatively modest number of outcomes, they are first distributed evenly across the space horizontally. Place outcomes with the least solution ambiguity on the right and the greatest solution ambiguity on the left.
2. Keeping horizontal positions fixed, move outcomes along a vertical axis, the outcome most visible to the customer at the top and least visible at the bottom.
3. Having spread out outcomes in two dimensions, we now have the space to draw the relationships between them—as with Plan on a Page, relationships of antecedence, impact, or leverage (see Figure 11).

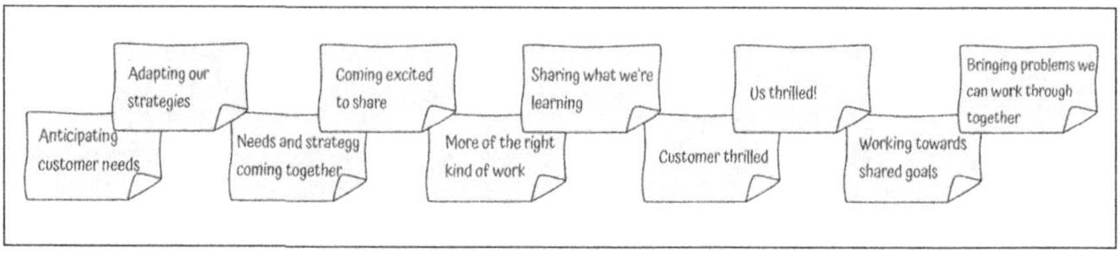

Figure 10: Option Relationship Mapping: initial horizontal distribution

In common with the Four Points exercise but this time just because it is efficient to do it this way, extreme examples serve to define the space:

1. For that initial spread across the horizontal axis of solution ambiguity, start with your most extreme examples—two from each breakout, their outcomes with the most and least solution ambiguity—and place them on the left and right sides, respectively, halfway up vertically (this will make the vertical distribution easier later); then distribute the rest evenly in between across the middle of the space.
2. For the vertical spread—remembering to keep horizontal positions fixed—again start by choosing extreme examples to go top and bottom, the outcomes with the greatest and least visibility to the customer; move the remainder up or down the customer visibility axis to achieve an even vertical distribution.

In both cases, "extreme" is relative. You might worry that some challenges and their outcomes might seem remote from the customer. Nevertheless, outcomes will be visible to varying degrees, and in practice, separating them is rarely difficult. As we saw in previous chapters, IdOO inquiries habitually converge on customer outcomes. Typically, these points of convergence are highly ambiguous, too.

Towards the right, where solution ambiguity is relatively low, solution choices may be limited by policy or consensus. So long as viable options remain, this need not be an obstacle. In Cynefin's terms, if the approach is clear to all, go with that! At the extreme left, where ambiguity is high, reminiscent of Cynefin's chaos domain, there may be a sense of being at a loss to know where to start. For outcomes further back from that extreme, it may still be apparent that much is to be done and much to be learned.

In the finished Options Relationship Map (Figure 11), even without reading what's written on the stickies, some interesting features may be discernible:

- Some outcomes *("Sharing what we're learning,"* for example) seem to play a pivotal role, with multiple relationships, both incoming and outgoing
- Although the majority of arrows point upward, enough point downward to raise the possibility of cycles—virtuous circles perhaps (For example, sharing what we're learning →needs and strategy coming together→more of the right kind of work→us thrilled→coming excited to share→sharing what we're learning)

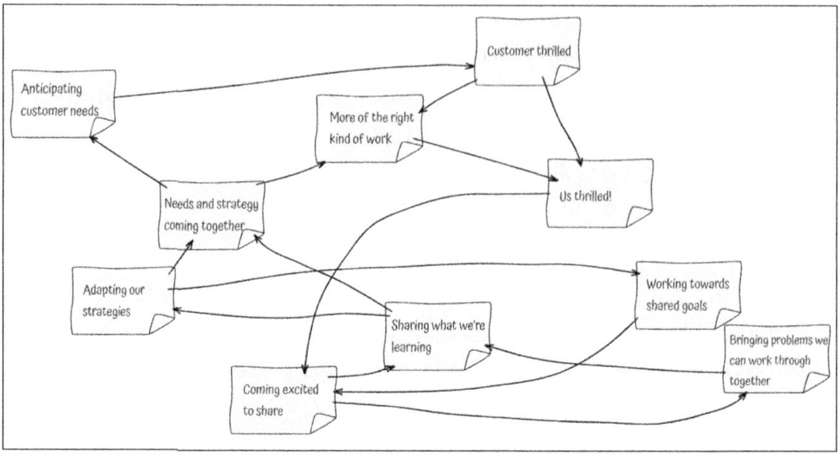

Figure 11 A completed Option Relationship Map

Virtuous circles beg a couple of questions:

- How might we get it started?
- What's stopping it from being a runaway success already?

With or without virtuous circles, the group is equipped to make some choices. Working backward from outcomes broadly shared as objectives, where might we start? Notice that with no loss of coherence, this question may have many answers—there is opportunity for everyone.

PART THREE

Generative Processes

SIX

Ideation and Experimentation

In terms of the Generative Change model, we are at this point well prepared to *engage diverse stakeholders in generative conversations and stimulate self-organized innovations (probes)*. They may feel more than ready—solution ideas have likely been bubbling under the surface for a while now. Now it's time to get what ideas they have out into the open and to help them generate plenty more.

The sheer volume and any possible impatience aside, what makes this a good time to move forward from inquiry into generative conversations is:

- There has been meaningful and constructive engagement with the adaptive challenge.
- Implicitly or explicitly, they accept that a monolithic solution or an implementation-based approach is not the way forward.
- There may be competing diagnoses, hypotheses, and goals, but paradoxically, perhaps, they add to the sense that plenty can be done. The landscape is rich enough that there is opportunity for everyone, and the shared experience is deep enough that the conversation will continue formally and informally. This might be the most important "tell." If the inquiry has been meaningful enough that you know people will keep talking about it without formal meetings, you are where you want to be.

Taking stock, they have plenty of raw material at their disposal:

- Outcomes that represent goals, measures of progress, areas of opportunity, or focal points for action—some outcomes perhaps representing more than one of these things simultaneously

- Relationships between outcomes that bring a sense of coherence, even if they are no more substantial than hypotheses
- Concerning the customer relationship and the internal experience—two areas that seem ripe for improvement—our case study group is ready to generate action ideas.

It seems appropriate to start with some definitions. First, *self-organized* has two accepted meanings. With roots in the study of systems, its older meaning describes the tendency for systems to find new configurations for themselves, usually more efficient than the configurations they replace. More recently, it has become synonymous with *self-managing*, perhaps with a stronger sense that groups (formed emergently or otherwise) can determine their own goals. In the context of generative change, both definitions apply. We infer that the work of innovation is done best by the people closest to the problem—at whatever level of organization the problem makes its presence most felt—and that some of that innovation may lead to better structures, better processes, and so on.

And some smaller definitions:

- *Solution*: an answer or resolution to a problem ("an answer" rather than "the answer" because multiple solutions may be possible) and/or something that brings about (or takes us toward) an outcome
- *Innovation*: a novel solution, including the application of an existing solution outside its normal context (*exaptation*)
- *Hypothesis*: an untested proposition, for example, that one outcome leads to another or that a solution idea will help accomplish an outcome
- *Experiments* (plural, because we can't expect a single experiment to suffice): how a hypothesis is tested
- *Probes*: exploratory experiments
- *Insights*: what is inferred from conducting experiments

Solution and *innovation* overlap quite a bit; *innovation* has something of the quality of a value, not (I think) because we necessarily desire novelty, but for the presumed advantage that innovation brings. The line between *experiment* and *probe* is also blurry; I tend to use *experiment* if it's about a solution for which we expect success and *probe* when it's more about finding out what's going on.

Not every change needs to be framed as an experiment or pilot project, but if you are unsure, it is a safer default than the alternative. Reasons in favor:

1. If you're doing anything new, there will be learning opportunities; framing units of change as experiments maximizes those opportunities.
2. Where there's a risk of failure, the business and psychological impacts are lessened, making it more likely that people will engage.

It can be tempting to treat experiments as decisions that have already been made but with conditions attached. There may be a place for that, but it risks making decisions prematurely without adequately evaluating the available learning. Therefore, I prefer to keep the experiment design separate from the decision-making process and recommend using deliberately soft language when framing hypotheses. I use this template:

> We believe that *<change>* will result in *<meaningful outcome(s)>*. If successful, we might expect to see:
>
> – *<observable impact>*
>
> …
>
> – <observable impact>

That works for hypotheses at every scale. In this chapter, we will see them at two entirely different levels of detail:

1. The 'big hypotheses' of your Theory of Change
2. The 'small hypotheses' of more everyday innovation

Bridging those scales may come with *pilot* experiments that lead the way. Those participants who like structure will have all the structure they need, and so long as the process has energy, those keen to get on with innovating won't be disappointed either. Little here can't be done in a few minutes, and being brisk is good. What we want are solution ideas and plenty of them.

Your big hypotheses

What are the big hypotheses of the Theory of Change (or, if you prefer, your Agenda for Change) that are hopefully emerging from the group? One great way to find out is to give the hypothesis template to your breakout groups and invite them to complete it. Here it is again:

> We believe that *<change>* will result in *<meaningful outcome(s)>*. If successful, we might expect to see:
>
> – *<observable impact>*
>
> ...
>
> – <observable impact>

The first part should reflect outcomes generated (chapters 2 and 3) and organized (chapter 5) previously, beginning with something pivotal or otherwise significant and taking in some prominent surrounding structure. If appropriate, multiple outcomes can be referenced, for example:

> We believe that focusing on team accomplishments, customer needs, and psychological safety in our meetings will improve collaboration both inside and outside our meetings.

Each *<observable impact>* is also an outcome. Some may have been identified already, and others may not. Either way, it's interesting: either "supports" or "leads to" relationships are being reinterpreted as "indicates progress towards" relationships and arranged relative to other outcomes, or the generative process is continuing. Completing the example:

> If successful, we might expect to see:
>
> – More focus and energy in our meetings
>
> – More collaboration in and as result of our meetings
>
> – Team accomplishments celebrated
>
> – Customer satisfaction increased
>
> – Improved staff retention

Echoing some of the techniques of the previous chapter, I like to present them in what feels like a progression—a sense perhaps of Andy Grove's (1995) *"pacing ourselves to see that we're getting there."* Again, this is not to preclude early work on "later" outcomes but to hint at some internal structure that might be exploited. What, for example, is the relationship between increased customer satisfaction and improved staff retention? That juxtaposition alone might catalyze some new ideas.

Describing a hypothesis as a generative image might be a stretch, but you might try this generative exercise. Looking at it element by element, ask:

- In this one aspect, what first, tiniest signs might tell us that something interesting might be beginning to emerge?

And then:

- What small solutions might bring those about?

Yes, we are talking solutions now. Solutions after outcomes, outcomes before solutions—whether you frame that as a process sequence or principle, we are ready now to talk solutions.

Generating and refining solution ideas

Recall that in a generative change strategy, you would not need to bring more structure to solution ideas—you just want to launch as many pilot projects as possible. If you are using a high-engagement strategy (Bushe & Lewis, 2023) you need to develop solutions the group supports that will be proposed to others. In my experience, there are three things that can help a group sort through all the ideas to create proposals that will have an impact after their work is over: meaning, measures and methods.

This can be read in two ways, first as a generative pattern, a process to follow:

1. **Meaning**—focusing on what's important
2. **Measure**—how we'll know that we're winning
3. **Method**—new ideas and how we'll test them

It can also be read as two warnings, arguments in favor of the generative approach we are taking:

1. **Meaning before Measure:** Don't lead with metrics that aren't meaningful to people and might drive dysfunctional behavior (Drucker disowned Management by Objectives with good reason)
2. **Measure before Method:** Don't choose solutions (let alone

implement them) without first defining how success will be measured; this is about finding solutions, not selling them, and by identifying multiple measures of success, we create additional affordances, increasing thereby the range of solution ideas

There is plenty of scope for using this simple pattern with some familiar tools. If, for example, you begin step 2 with your "first, tiniest signs," you could be practicing Solutions Focus. Alternatively, you might use the meaning, measure method pattern to guide a Challenge Mapping session.

Here, for Meaning and Measure, I'll illustrate this by using the IdOO pattern, using Ideal and Obstacles for Meaning, and Outcomes for Measure. Choose an outcome that we want to work with:

1. **Ideal:** Envision it working at its ideal best, reminding ourselves why it's important to us, using stories to enrich our understanding of what it can do for whom
2. **Obstacles:** The usual questions—*What stops us? What gets in the way? Why is that important?*
3. **Outcomes:** How will we recognize that good things are beginning to emerge? How will we know that we're making meaningful progress? How will we know that we're winning?

Then Method:

4. **Solution options:** Plenty of them, and as diverse as we can make them
5. **'Fantastic' and 'intriguing' options:** Not to exclude options prematurely, but to uncover hidden assumptions
6. **Parallel probes:** If you are taking many ideas forward

Notice that steps 1-4 are *divergent*, expanding the thinking, increasing the search space, and generating new ideas. Much less obviously, there is a divergent aspect even to step 5; later that will become explicit.

The Meaning, Measure, Method process is not about analysis or decision-making; it's about making the search space richer, increasing the abundance and diversity of solution options, and increasing the chances of overall success. In the more detailed description that follows, keep in mind that the host keeps the process moving swiftly. This is not the time to get bogged down! In step 4, the process should remain energized, and as many preceding conversations as possible should stay in the air. Especially if each breakout can see a reminder of the process and the questions asked, steps 1-4 can be completed as a single exercise lasting only a few minutes.

Meaning (I): Ideal

If doing this for the first time (immediately after a Mapping exercise, perhaps) and breakout groups haven't already chosen an outcome they want to work on, you can prime them for learning by selecting an "*interesting*" outcome. That means interesting not only in the sense that they are motivated to act on it, but that it is moderately ambiguous, not so ambiguous that it's difficult to know where to start, nor so unambiguous that to use an ideation process of any kind might seem overkill. Alternatively, now could be the opportunity for forming new breakout groups by people moving to the outcome they want to work on.

For their chosen outcome, you might ask:

- *Why is that important?*
- When it's working at its ideal best:
  - *Whose needs would we be meeting?*
  - *What new stories could they tell?*

"*What new stories could they tell?*" invites *job stories*. Recall from chapter 2 that these contain or strongly imply two elements:

1. A *struggling moment* or *authentic situation of need*—the when and where of a scenario in which a need arises
2. The *meaningful progress* made when that need was met

Moving swiftly on while this is all fresh...

Meaning (II): Obstacles

We're interested here more in quantity than quality, so we won't be doing a formal Obstacles Fast and Slow review step. Nevertheless, some reminders:

1. Obstacles that judge or blame won't help you find solutions that are within your power

2. Obstacles that sell solutions or theories may distract you and others from finding better solutions

With those warnings out of the way and concerning the ideal:

- What stops that? What gets in the way? Why is that important?

Measure: Outcomes

With respect again to the *'ideal best'* outcome and all its detail (now including obstacles) and working our way up from the smallest outcomes:

- What first, tiniest signs might tell us that something interesting might be beginning to emerge?
- How will we know we've made a small but significant step in the right direction?
- How will we measure real success?
- What would 'fantastic' look like?

Method

At last, solutions! With some variations on *How might we…?*, the goal here is to generate a good selection of ideas for various levels of experimentation:

- *How might we* learn more about what's possible?
- *How might we* test our understanding in a way likely to yield some useful business benefit, overcoming an obstacle perhaps?
- *How might we* make meaningful progress towards our chosen outcome or outcomes that are supportive of it?

One significant variation in this step is to combine it with what might be Liberating Structures' most famous pattern, 1-2-4-All (Lipmanowicz & McCandless, 2014) . Possibly skipping the '2' step (pairwise conversations) if you're online:

1: Generation

Individually (silently), generate solution ideas that are as diverse as you can make them. Some tips to increase diversity:

- If your first idea involves new tools, try to think of one that doesn't
- If your first idea has people outside your team taking the lead, try to think of one where you take responsibility instead—(here, you might emphasize the "*we*" in "*How might we…?*")
- What would experts from different backgrounds recommend?

Inspired by Solutions Focus:

- What has worked elsewhere?
- What is already beginning to work here?

And via Liberating Structures, channeling Gareth Morgan (see Morgan & Zohar, 1995):

- What's your *15% solution*? Putting aside the 85% that's beyond your control, what is the 15% there for the taking?

2: Pairwise refinement

In pairs, quickly explain and refine your ideas. Which ideas do you want to carry forward? As you bring your ideas together, what new ideas are triggered?

4: Group consolidation

In a similar vein, bring your ideas together in your breakout group. Which ideas do you want to share? As you bring your ideas together, what new ideas are triggered? What do they look like in combination?
All: Debrief

In the 'All' part, breakouts share their best ideas, again with the possibility of recombination. Especially if doing this for the first time, don't forget to debrief the exercise experience so that participants can better repeat it unsupported. By habit, my debriefs usually start there; do make sure, however, that solution ideas get the attention they're due.

'Fantastic' and 'intriguing' options

Which of these ideas should be taken forward? That's a good question; there are so many different methods by which you could try to answer it. In the context of generative change, the obvious correct answer is to choose ideas that people are already motivated to try. Still, given the ability of many organizations to kill good ideas at birth, we'll explore ways to make them more robust.

Another question then:

- What would have to be true for this option to look fantastic?

This one isn't mine; it's from Roger L. Martin, former Dean of the Rotman School of Management at the University of Toronto. I found it in *Playing to Win*, (Lafley & Martin, 2013; Lafley is the former CEO of Proctor & Gamble). We'll take it in two parts, the "*fantastic*" part and the "what would have to be true" part, the latter of which makes it a question about assumptions and dependencies.

First, consider each action idea's 'best case scenario' (your options). Can they be "*fantastic*," delivering benefits in learning and/or other more direct forms of business value that significantly outweigh the costs involved?

For your more promising action ideas, identify and discuss the things that would need to be true for that option to deliver that hoped-for degree of upside. This list may include:

- Things under your control
- Things that you will come to depend on later
- Things that you're not sure of at this time but could perhaps find out
- Things that will always be hard to predict
- Things that may remain essentially unknowable until the last (or worst) moment

How fantastic do your options look after you have accounted for their likelihood of success? You might characterize them as solid and boring (not likely to be fantastic, but still reliable), exciting but risky (high potential, but perhaps more likely to fail than to succeed), or not worth the trouble (little to no chance of success). If you generate enough ideas against enough outcomes, you'll soon have a good mixture—a healthy 'options portfolio,' if you like—even after eliminating the duds.

A second approach is to look for "*intriguing*" options. Like the "*interesting*" outcomes we saw earlier in the chapter, intriguing solution ideas are attractive and non-obvious but not so "out there" that it's difficult to hypothesize their impact. These are likely to be the solution ideas most capable of generating learning for the organization and defensible on that basis.

If you are doing this for the first time and want to try framing solution ideas as hypotheses, these should be great candidates. Much as before:

> We believe that *<solution idea>* will result in *<meaningful outcome(s)>*. If successful, we might expect to see:
>
> – *<observable impact>*
>
> …
>
> – *<observable impact>*

Parallel probes

You will likely still have multiple solution options in front of you at this stage. What do you do? Maintain focus by trying only one solution idea at a time, or try to make progress on multiple fronts?

In practice—and this is reassuring if, like me, you have been trained not to exceed your capacity—this problem is largely self-limiting. Self-organized probes aren't just ideas on paper; they are ideas people have organized around and are motivated to act on and learn from. Only so many ideas will be taken forward at this point.

A couple of words of general advice, though:

1. Don't start what you can't finish
2. Don't start what will interfere with something else

When you start what you can't finish, you consume capacity without having anything to show for it. To avoid that, break larger ideas down into things that can be achieved quickly. That isn't to create a detailed plan to follow but to enable rapid progress on ideas small enough that their delay-inducing dependencies are much easier to see.

The advice on interfering is sensible, but it isn't absolute. Borrowing from Cynefin, if you don't know where to start (a strong indicator of ambiguity) or if you have competing hypotheses (which you can take as encouraging evidence of sophistication), test the waters with parallel probes. Given that they can't all be right, you want probes to be quick, safe, and cheap. Even if results can't be interpreted unambiguously, if they help to identify a promising way forward, that's a win.

Closing thoughts: Layers of generativity

We've come quite a long way in this chapter—from outcomes to hypotheses, experiments, solution ideas, and even some operational advice—but the most striking thing about it might be its familiarity. The Ideal, Obstacles, Outcomes pattern did half the work of the ideation process, and within that pattern, we've seen many of the questions before.

If done well, people will feel energized and hopeful that good things will happen. The process of inquiry, then generativity, makes sense. They know where they are in the process. They feel a personal commit-ment to the outcomes under discussion. They feel included and have some sense of agency. Collaborative relationships and processes have strengthened amongst them. They are ready to talk about solutions, and whatever emerges will likely be in the service of agreed outcomes.

Add the Meaning, Measure, Method pattern, and you will have over-lapping structures you can easily keep in your head. You can use these inside or outside a workshop environment with the questions provided here or with your own.

So, after several chapters of deferring, deflecting, or glossing over the talk of solutions, this was indeed the chapter of outcomes before solu-tions, outcomes as the catalyst for solutions, and solutions identified by people who are already motivated to test them.

The challenge is to extract the learning promised by that testing and sustain the process. Unfortunately, one experiment does not inevitably lead to another. The following and final chapter will focus on what can be done about that.

SEVEN

Keeping the Conversation Alive

In the previous chapter, we left our group generating and refining solution ideas in two key areas: the customer relationship (which had been poor) and the internal experience (likewise). Some participants may have felt more drawn to one of those areas than the other. Still, both had people motivated to make changes, and everyone understood that the two areas were related. Now, the challenge is to sustain their work for long enough not only to see some initial results but also for those first changes to bed in, for further progress to build on those gains, and ultimately for the work to gain momentum.

In the words of the Generative Change Model, they have been *engaging diverse stakeholders in generative conversations* and *stimulating self-organized innovations (probes)*. But the model does not stop there, and neither should they! In this closing chapter, we have two final steps to consider:

- Learn from successes and failures
- Scale up and embed successful probes

Stepping back for a moment, this book has emphasized agreement on outcomes as the basis for focusing ideas for change. It is as though we have kept asking the following questions:

1. What if we put *agreement on outcomes* before solutions?

That is Agendashift's principle #1 framed (as I like to do) in the form of a question. Now, and in a similar vein:

2. How do we keep bringing outcomes to the foreground?
   - Where—and where else—could we be doing this?

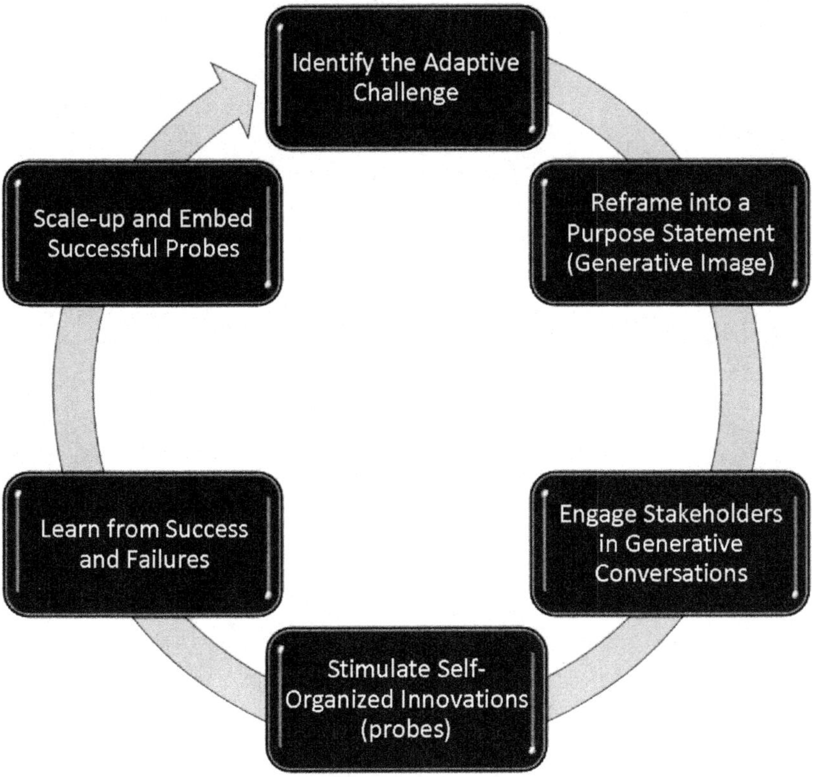

Figure 12. The Generative Change Model

We are building on the desire to move the conversation into its next phase, making progress through experimentation and effecting some real change. But raising our sights higher, we want to reach a point where the ongoing process is generative because it creates at least as many ideas as it consumes.

Why aim that high? Quite simply because most change initiatives run out of steam long before they achieve their objectives. However inclusive or inspiring the process, objective setting rarely suffices. Nothing is inevitable about experimentation continuing in cycles. If it does continue, and especially if it feels like there's something iterative about it, then there must be something sustaining it. To keep sponsors and others whose support they need engaged, we have to ensure the meaningfulness of the outcomes being pursued, matched by the meaningfulness of the process used to pursue them.

To address that sustainability challenge, two more patterns:

1. **Right to Left**—working backward from critical moments of impact and learning
2. **Thinking in Circles**—whatever the scope of the original generative challenge, recognizing that inside it, outside it, adjacent to it, and overlapping with it, there are likely other scopes with their related challenges

Together, these patterns help us close the loop of the Generative Change Model (Figure 12) in an exciting way. This is not merely as iteration—refreshing the strategy when a point of diminishing returns is reached—but as something reproductive. As learning happens, there is the opportunity to build on and spread it. The change process produces new instances of itself, engaging deeply with the organization's complexity and becoming an integral part of it. This change in organizational culture creates a more agile, adaptive organization.

Right to Left

Part pattern, part metaphor, Right to Left means working backward from two key moments. I allude to them in a subversive twist to a concept popular in Agile circles, the *definition of done*. My definition:

- **Done** (adj) /dʌn/
  Someone's need was met.
- **Really done** *(adj) /ˈrɪəli dʌn/*
  We've accounted for the learning.

Those two key moments—the moment of impact, when we can prove the outcome we've aimed for has happened, and the moment of learning, when that accounting is done—beg some questions. Several of these will have been asked before, but they're worth asking again:

- Whose need?
- What need?
- How would we know that we've met that need?
- By what means do we plan to meet that need?
- What do we expect to learn in the process?
- How prepared are we for a surprise?
- How confident can we be in that learning?

There can be many opportunities to ask those questions, which could be described as "everyday" feedback opportunities and more formal and longer-cadence review meetings. In the former, conversations reduce ambiguity, enhance shared understanding through clarification and reiteration, and encourage more stories of need, struggle, and fulfillment to be told. In the latter, the learning is consolidated, informing future decisions. I'll describe how the Right to Left pattern applies at both levels.

Everyday feedback opportunities

The origins of *Right to left* as a visual metaphor are in a Lean practice called *Kanban* (see Burrows, 2014). As pioneered by Toyota on the automotive production line, one important way to keep the amount of work-in-progress under control on the factory floor is to have each work item—each car produced, each of its constituent subassemblies, and small batches of supplies—represented by visual tokens or cards, the kanban. By carefully limiting the numbers of those kanban in circulation at any time, over-supply, over-production, and overburdening are eliminated, eliminating needless self-inflicted delay and achieving smooth, fast, *just-in-time* production.

In knowledge work, of which generative change is a fascinating example, we don't see cards moving around the factory floor. We can, however, achieve much the same effect with sticky notes or cards on a whiteboard limited in number by policy or practice. Kanban board designs can vary widely according to the process designs they visualize and the range of visualization techniques employed, but typically, they feature columns for each activity or work item state, arranged left-to-right in the process's natural sequence.

The Changeban board (Figure 13) is a kanban board designed for running experiments. In the Changeban game (agendashift.com/changeban) we simulate a mix of product and organizational experiments, an identical process for both but distinguishing between those two kinds of work by sticky note color.

The term *right to left* originates in how we review the board. We start from the right with experiments (or, more generally, work) that's recently finished or closest to being finished and working backwards from there. That simple practice helps in several ways:

Changeban

Agree Urgency	In progress ( )			Complete ☺
	Negotiate Change ( )	Validate Adoption ( )	Verify Performance ( )	
				Accepted
				Rejected AU ¦ NC ¦ VA ¦ VP
Is it **valuable**? Will we get to it soon?	Is it **feasible**? Is it acceptable to all parties?	Is it **usable**? Will it stick?	Is it *proving* **valuable**? Is it meeting needs?	

Figure 13. The Changeban board

- We're focussed first on finishing
- We're concentrated next on what is or isn't progressing through the process
- At the beginning of the process, we avoid starting work for which we lack the capacity

About individual cards, I use words like "experiment," "change," "idea," and "solution" as seems fitting; in other contexts, words such as "work," "work item," or "feature" might be appropriate (less so "task," typically associated more with the activity than the outcome). Imagine now a recurring review of the board and the questions that might go with each column:

- **Complete** (covering both accepted and failed)
  - Are these experiments staying done?
  - What are we still learning from them?
  - What further follow-ups are required?
- **Verify performance**
  - What do we know about how these changes are performing?

  - What do we still need to do/find out/measure to get them over the line?

- **Validate adoption**
  - Compared to expectations, how well are these changes being taken up?
  - What are our first impressions of these changes in use?
  - Are we seeing any unforeseen problems that we need to resolve?

- **Negotiate change**
  - How confident are we in the feasibility and acceptability of our solution?
  - Who has participated in its design?

- **Agree urgency**
  - When we have the capacity, what comes next?
  - Why this item over the others?

Capacity permitting, those last two questions may spawn separate conversations to ensure that each new item gets off to a good start. In these and subsequent board reviews, until any possible doubt has been eliminated, the *done* and *really done* questions are useful:

- Whose need?
- What need?
- How would we know that we've met that need?
- What do we expect to learn in the process?
- How prepared are we for surprise?
- How confident can we be in that learning?

Some might find it strange that I've described a quick meeting called to kick off a piece of work as a feedback opportunity and not a handover. But the work up to this point is the product of a participatory process! Those doing the work and/or impacted by it should be well represented already, and the collaboration needn't stop when the workshops end.

Hosts (and leaders generally) should not be afraid to repeat themselves daily; do so for long enough, and the routines become not just theirs and deliberate but shared and automatic. Notice the outcome-before-solution sequence: we don't ask *"by what means"* until the need has been explored, it's clear to everyone what we're working towards, and we've determined how we'll know we've achieved it. This way, the outcome still stands if the solution does not work.

It is worth noting how open this "everyday" process is to surprise. Working in right-to-left order again:

- Items don't always stay 'done' (one reason for keeping them on the board)
- We might learn from recently completed work even when its 'done-ness' is not in question
- 'Done' or not, it might not be performing as expected
- The intended users of our ideas might not be as eager as we expected
- The solution might not be as feasible as we thought
- To those who have a say in the matter, the solution might be as acceptable as we hoped (perhaps with hindsight, those people weren't involved early enough)
- What seemed like a great idea wasn't going to be worth the effort

We don't make the mistake of assuming that what looks good on paper must work in practice if it is specified and scrutinized rigorously enough and implemented robustly enough. Instead, we use a process much better suited to an adaptive challenge that tries to ask the right questions at the right time, ideas increasingly tested against reality, unnecessary waste and pain minimized. Compared to pushing a doomed solution to completion, setbacks can be regarded as minor, and each is an opportunity for reflection and ideation.

With all this opportunity for feedback, there's every chance that ideas are generated faster than they can be consumed. Not only is that a helpful working definition of a generative process, but it's also a key ingredient in making the overall change process self-sustaining.

If a Dialogic OD process lacks suitable feedback opportunities and you fail to make them a priority, then the consequences are clear. The right questions will be asked less often, well-intended but doomed solutions will be pushed further than they should, ideas will slow to a trickle, and if it's maintained at all, progress overall will be slower.

I'm not about to argue for a prescriptive change, however. Keeping faith with participation and self-organization, we'll deal with this issue by working backward and asking another of my favorite questions: *Who's invited?*

Longer-cadence feedback opportunities

Take yourself to the end of your initial workshop. Instead of assigning actions to people (anathema in a generative change process), imagine that a change process is already underway: by engaging in the inquiry and solution finding, the "informal" organization is shifting on its own. Now step forward in time to your first review, where you're celebrating the excellent progress that has already been made, agreeing on adjustments in the light of recent experience, and looking forward eagerly to the following review.

Question: *Who's invited?*

The best answer is "everyone affected," but if that's not feasible, let me paint a picture of how review meetings can work. This is not to be prescriptive but to give you an example of whether there's room for improvement in meetings already in place.

I call this a Strategy Performance and Alignment Review (SPAR). The objectives are:

- To see what we can do to make our reviews more outside-in (start with the customers), with implications for the top-level agenda, for who participates, and for alignment
- To see what we can do to make our reviews more right-to-left—focussed on impact and learning and designed to keep workload well matched to capacity—that *just-in-time* philosophy applied to the learning process

That right-left-left philosophy applies even to the smallest of these meetings. Updates work backward from objectives. Here's a structure I like to use:

- Objectives—what the people giving the update are trying to achieve
- Measures of success—how well they are doing and how they know

- Experiments concluded since last time - what has been learned from them, and their consequences
- Experiments soon to complete - how they're going, and what's outstanding
- Other experiments in progress and what we expect from them
- What's next and why

Subject to the courtesy of not dropping items between reviews without explanation, representatives are trusted to make sensible choices about the level and amount of detail reported. Continuity is quickly established, and meetings gain a level and momentum of their own. They can even be identity-forming.

Replace "experiments" with "work" or "issues," and you have a protocol worth considering for almost any kind of progress review. However, when the goal is learning, it pays to put some extra effort into reviewing those recently completed items. Some possible questions:

- What assumptions were you testing?
- Which of those held true?
- Which of those were invalidated?
- What was inconclusive?
- What other surprises arose?
- What improvements to the experiment's design or conduct might have caused the above information to be generated sooner?
- In light of that, what changes to the strategy or our process should we consider making?

To that last question, I sometimes joke that no meeting is more ironically named than the "lessons learned" meeting. If nothing changes, what learning has really occurred?

You may find this little template helpful:

We thought <*assumption*> but instead found <*result*>.

Had we <*alternative*>, we might have discovered this sooner.

As a result, <*change*>.

If the review is big enough for participation or content to benefit from some high-level structure, try starting with the group or theme closest to the customer. One possible agenda follows that of the Outside-in Strategy Review:

1. Customer
2. Organization
3. Product
4. Platform
5. Team(s)

I conducted my first experiments with this structure in a UK government digital setting. There, those five updates were given by:

1. The product owner and the user researcher, speaking to customer-related issues and incorporating updates from the customer support desk
2. The service manager and the product owner giving updates from the wider organization and taking issues back
3. The product owner again, this time speaking to progress on the digital service's product strategy
4. The tech lead and the "DevOps" representative (the latter spanning development and technology operations), speaking to the technology platform, its development, and its performance
5. The delivery manager (me), speaking to people and process more generally.

That worked so much better than just going around the room, where the sequence resulted from nothing more meaningful than seating position. Reviewing progress in that outside-in sequence made any misalignment glaringly obvious if our aspirations for our customers and the organization (very much in that order) weren't supported in subsequent updates. Happily, where the mantra was *"Start with needs: user needs, not government needs,"* this sequence felt very natural.

Thinking in circles

Let's relook at the outside-in strategy review, this time in terms of who the participants represented:

1. The product team, which comprised the product owner and the user researcher, plus a business analyst and a user experience designer who had feet in both the product team and the technology team; also (indirectly, via the product owner's update), the customer support desk
2. The government agency's wider digital organization, the employer of the service manager (who, despite being the most senior participant present, went second in these meetings, not first), and the product team (consultants held most other roles)
3. The product team again
4. The technology team and various groups involved in production support
5. All of the above as a team, and myself—me there not as manager but as host

Looking back on that very positive experience, I came to identify a *"rule of three"* for those significant feedback opportunities—including, I believe, generative change events:

- Have at least three levels of seniority present for any significant feedback opportunity

That gives you:

1. Authority, strategic context, and where necessary, budget
2. First-hand, front-line knowledge
3. The perspective of those whose job is often to bridge the other two perspectives coherently

At the time, I was unaware of Ackoff's "up a level, down two levels, back up a level" kind of *synthesis* (Ackoff, 1999), but there is definitely some resonance. Even later, I came to recognize that together with certain cultural aspects, the wide range of seniorities participating combined with the pairing of colleagues in their updates mirrored a Sociocratic structure (Buck & Villenes, 2019):

1. People organized in *circles* responsible and accountable for a particular *domain*

2. Decisions made within circles by consent, including (as was the case here) the membership of those circles
3. Especially in governance relationships, *double linking* between circles, not just (say) a team leader in the intersections between circles, but two people, enhancing representation in both directions and often creating opportunities for personal development

The meeting's participants formed a governance circle for our project, doubly linked to each team and the broader organization.

I didn't set out to implement Sociocracy (aka Dynamic Governance, or per Ackoff, Circular Hierarchy) as the project's governance model, but once I noticed how well it described what we did, I have never looked at organizing in quite the same way since.

Letting process and governance take more credit than they deserve would be mistaken and unfair. Focusing on the people present, those they represent, and the potential for their generative journey is much better. On behalf of their circles and then with them, each might ask themselves:

- What is our identity? Could it be more robust?
- What is our purpose? Could it be more explicit?
- What is our adaptive challenge, a challenge we're the right people to own?
- What's it like when it's all working at its ideal best for us?
- What stops that? What gets in the way?
- What would we like to have happen?

The picture I'd like to leave you with isn't just one strategy but a web of strategies. If you can see your context as a circle, how much can you achieve if everything around you is fixed? Wouldn't change be easier to sustain if it's also happening in smaller circles within your context, in circles adjacent to yours or overlapping, and in scopes encompassing yours? And wouldn't it be easier still if there were some accounting for the impact and learning between those circles?

Closing thoughts: Grasping the opportunity

In the process of change—generative or otherwise—there are typically many kinds of leaders involved:

- Sponsors opening the door to change and lending support both moral and financial
- Managers of the divisions, departments, products, and services impacted
- Leaders of teams balancing the work of change with the ever-present work of production
- Those from inside or outside the organization lending their expertise or supporting the process as coaches or hosts

And for each of those roles, multiple 'hats':

- "Keeper of context," alert to every participant's need for context so that good decisions can be made and great work done—not just providing it but seeking to improve the organization so that context is available when and where it's needed
- Client, appropriately descriptive about goals and challenges
- Coach, helping participants experience moments of insight
- Host, ensuring that others enjoy a productive time—attending to what's happening and to the environment that it occurs in, providing appropriate boundaries

If any of those seemed abstract or only for the big occasion, it should be apparent now that the opportunities for inquiry and generative conversation are many and varied. 'Everyday' might even understate the scale of that opportunity! With a range of well-sized experiments and other work items at various stages of progress, every day, there will be multiple opportunities to use the prompts and questions of this chapter or those of your own.

What might at first feel repetitive would better be regarded as a change in narratives or culture: leadership routines becoming part of the leader's language and those around them. The language and its development reflect shared understandings of the nature of the process (needs-based, outcome-oriented, participatory, generative), the process itself (its goals, steps, methods, and so on), how it performs, and how it evolves.

That is what makes generative change so exciting. What are you left with at the end of a traditional change initiative? When it's done, it's done, and you live with the consequences, good and bad. Through the process, generative change creates many more opportunities for leadership in many more places, and if just a few people grasp those opportunities, the organization is changing for the better already.

References

agilemanifesto (2001). *Manifesto for Agile Software Development.* agilemanifesto.org.

Ackoff, R.L. (1999). *Re-Creating the Corporation: A Design of Organizations for the 21st Century.* OUP USA.

Averbuch, T. (2021). *Initiating and Inviting Generative Change: Entry and Contracting for Emergent Outcomes in Results-Driven Organizations.* BMI.

Banfield, R., Lombardo, C.T., & Wax, T. (2015). *Design Sprint: A Practical Guidebook for Building Great Digital Products.* O'Reilly Media.

Barrett, F. J., Thomas, G. F., & Hocevar, S. P. (1995). The central role of discourse in large-scale change: A social construction perspective. *The Journal of Applied Behavioral Science, 31*(3), 352-372.

Basadur, M. (2003). *Reducing Complexity in Conceptual Thinking Using Challenge Mapping.* ResearchGate.

Bateson, G. (1972). *Steps to an Ecology of Mind.* University of Chicago Press.

Buck, J & Villenes, S. (2019). *We the People: Consenting to a Deeper Democracy.* Sociocracy (2nd Ed.). Info Press.

Burrows, M. (2014). *Kanban from the Inside.* Blue Hole Press.

Burrows, M. (2017). *A True North for Lean-Agile?* (blog.agendashift.com/2017/05/22/a-true-north-for-lean-agile/)

Burrows, M. (2019). *Right to Left: The Digital Leader's Guide to Lean and Agile.* New Generation Publishing.

Burrows, M. (2021). *Agendashift: Outcome-Oriented Change And Continuous Transformation (2nd Ed.).* New Generation Publishing.

Bushe, G. (2020). *The Dynamics of Generative Change.* BMI.

Bushe, G.R. & Lewis, S. (2023). Three change strategies in organization development: Data-based, high engagement, and generative. *Leadership and Organization Development Journal, 44*(2), 173–188.

Bushe, G.R. & Marshak, R.J. (Eds.). (2015) *Dialogic Organization Development: The Theory and Practice of Transformational Change.* Berrett-Koehler.

Bushe, G. R., & Nagaishi, M. (2018). Imagining the future through the past: Organization development isn't (just) about change. *Organization Development Journal, 36*(3), 23-36.

Cameron, K.S. & Quinn, R.B. (2011). *Diagnosing and Changing Organizational Culture: Based on the Competing Values Framework.* Jossey-Bass.

Cooperrider, D. L., & Srivastava, S. (1987). Appreciative inquiry in organizational life. *Research in Organizational Change and Development, 1*, 129-169.

Eaton, M. (2010). Why change programs fail. *Human Resource Management International Digest, 18*(2), 37-42.
Grove, A. (1995) *High Output Management.* Vintage Books.
Hastings, B. J., & Schwarz, G. M. (2022). Leading change processes for success: a dynamic application of diagnostic and dialogic organization development. *The Journal of Applied Behavioral Science, 58*(1), 120-148.
Hohmann, L. (2006). *Innovation Games: Creating Breakthrough Products Through Collaborative Play.* Pearson Education.
Johnson, B. (2020). *And: Making a Difference by Leveraging Polarity, Paradox or Dilemma.* Human Resource Development Press.
Jackson, P. & McKergow, M. (2011). *The Solutions Focus: Making Coaching and Change SIMPLE.* Nicholas Brealey International.
Juarrero, A. (2023). *Context Changes Everything: How Constraints Create Coherence.* The MIT Press.
Kaner, S. (2007). *Facilitator's Guide to Participatory Decision-Making.* Jossey Bass.
Klein, G. (2007). Performing a project premortem. *Harvard Business Review, 85*(9), 18-19.
Lafley, A.G. & Martin, R.L. (2013). *Playing to Win: How Strategy Really Works.* Harvard Business Review Press.
Lewis, S. (2024). *Creating Energized Commitment to the Dialogic Approach: The Change Team's Journey of Discovery.* BMI.
Lipmanowicz, H. & McCandless, K. (2014). *The Surprising Power of Liberating Structures: Simple Rules to Unleash A Culture of Innovation.* Liberating Structures Press.
McKergow, M. (2020). *Hosting Generative Change: Creating Containers for Creativity and Commitment.* BMI.
Mezick, D. & Sheffield, M. (2018). *Inviting Leadership: Invitation-Based Change™ in the New World of Work.* FreeStanding Press.
Mintzberg, H. (1994). *The Rise and Fall of Strategic Planning.* Prentice Hall.
Moesta, B. & Engle, G. (2020). *Demand-Side Sales 101: Stop Selling and Help Your Customers Make Progress.* Lioncrest Publishing.
Morgan, G., & Zohar, A. (1995). *Achieving Quantum Change Incrementally!!: The Art of High Leverage Change.* York University.
Mosadeghrad, A.M. & Ansarian, M. (2014). Why do organisational change programmes fail? *International Journal of Strategic Change Management, 5*(3), 189-218.
Noonan, R. (2007). *Discussing the Undiscussable: A Guide to Overcoming Defensive Routines in the Workplace.* Jossey-Bass.
Patton, J. & Economy, P. (2014). *User Story Mapping: Discover the Whole Story, Build the Right Product.* O'Reilly Media.
Shook, J. (2008). *Managing to Learn: Using the A3 Management Process to Solve Problems, Gain Agreement, Mentor, and Lead.* Lean Enterprise Institute.
Smith. K.K. & Berg, D.N. (1987). *Paradoxes of Group Life.* Jossey-Bass

Snowden, D. J., & Boone, M. E. (2007). A leader's framework for decision making. *Harvard Business Review, 85*(11), 68-76.

Snowden, D. J. & Quinlan, T. (2018) *The Future, Backwards.* (cynefin.io/wiki/Future_backwards)

Sullivan, W. & Rees, J (2008). *Clean Language: Revealing Metaphors and Opening Minds.* Crown House Publishing.

Towers Watson (2013). Towers Watson change and communication ROI survey. Retrieved from https://www.towerswatson.com/ en/Press/2013/08/Only-One-Quarter-of- Employers-Are-Sustaining-Gains-From-Change-Management

Van de Ven, A. H. (1986). Central problems in the management of innovation. *Management Science, 32*(5), 590-607.

Walker, C. (2014). *From Contempt to Curiosity: Creating the Conditions for Groups to Collaborate Using Clean Language and Systemic Modelling.* Clean Publishing.

Way, M. (2013). *Clean Approaches for Coaches: How to Create the Conditions for Change Using Clean Language and Symbolic Modelling.* Clean Publishing.

Weick, K. (1979, 1969). *The Social Psychology of Organizing.* McGraw-Hill.

BMI Series in Dialogic OD

The BMI series in Dialogic OD, inspired by the original Addison-Wesley Series in OD, is a series of short, 100-page volumes about various aspects of change leadership written by experienced Dialogic OD practitioners. Edited by Gervase Bushe, each narrowly focuses on one specific facet of Dialogic OD practice and provides consultants with tested, practical models and processes, along with case examples, to make the models come alive. All are available through Amazon.

For more information on the authors and to read testimonials, visit https://b-m-institute.com.

Dialogic Process Consulting: Generative Meaning-Making in Action
https://b-m-institute.com/books/dialogic-process-consulting/

Robert Marshak introduces a subtle but powerful dialogic OD method that coaches and consultants can use to help clients address limiting assumptions and create new possibilities. The phrase "generative meaning-making in action" captures the essence of the approach. You will learn how to identify and address out-of-awareness mindsets during everyday conversations, how to deeply listen for the implicit mindsets that influence meaning-making in individuals, groups and organizations, and how to intervene through transforming talk to challenge or change them.

The Dynamics of Generative Change

https://b-m-institute.com/books/the-dynamics-of-generative-change/

Gervase Bushe steps you through the Generative Change Model, a way to approach organizational change more aligned with today's needs for an agile and engaged workforce than planned change methods. We follow the case of Consolidated Construction Materials Supply, 200 poorly engaged employees inside a large, traditional construction company. Organized into three fragmented units, this low-tech warehouse and distribution operation transformed into a highly engaged, collaborative, agile and fully digitized one in a little more than two years after the first phone call between the consultant and the Director. They accomplished this without a vision, without a plan, without training, any resistance to change, and only 1 external OD consultant. The book provides advice on the key issues in leading an emergent, generative change process. Many other books in the series assume the reader knows the generative change process.

Hosting Generative Change: Creating Containers for Creativity and Commitment

http://b-m-institute.com/books/hosting-generative-change/

When the future is uncertain and the past is contested, good hosting can bring hope and co-operation into the present. Any Dialogic OD practice will bring people together for creative conversations, expanded horizons, mutual connection and committed action. The way these events are hosted can make all the difference. **Mark McKergow** brings over a decade of research into the etiquette of hosting in different cultures and eras and combines it with three decades of practice in organizational development and change. The book offers an image of superb hosting as a mix of detailed planning and openness to whatever emerges, taking the lead when needed, with the intent of stepping back as quickly as possible so participants can lead themselves. The book offers a framework of six hosting roles to help navigate the inevitable ups and downs of working with large (and small) groups.

The Team Discovered: Dialogic Team Coaching

http://b-m-institute.com/books/the-team-discovered/

This hopeful, poignant, and deeply insightful book brings the wisdom of Dialogic OD and the heritage of Diagnostic OD into an expansive view of how to best support teams in a world of immense diversity and attention poverty. **Bennett Bratt** offers a new approach to team development that meets today's teams where they live: in a complex world with intense demands and precious little time. This book challenges widely used approaches to team development that utilize data showing a gap between current and desirable team performance. Most methods presume some kind of evaluative comparison is helpful: comparison to other groups, comparison to large data sets, comparison to best practices, comparison to a theoretical ideal. Instead, Ben explains why a dialogic approach to the use of questionnaire data is better at helping teams author their own narrative of effectiveness, one they will own and live into. While showing how to make data useful, Ben persuasively argues that comparison is at best, a distraction and at worst, debilitating. The book illustrates how to bring the mindsets and tools of Dialogic OD to team coaching through an extended case example.

From Physical Place to Virtual Space: How to Design and Host Transformative Events Online.

https://b-m-institute.com/books/from-physical-place-to-virtual-space/

Gwen Stirling-Wilkie describes the insights and conclusions of a highly experienced Dialogic Organization Development practitioner bringing her skills to a new client, all online. The book covers the differences that make a difference in doing Dialogic OD online in two parts. The first part (Preparing the Virtual Space) covers the changes we must make, and the new opportunities available, to how we normally design dialogic change processes to accommodate virtual space. Gwen identifies four different kinds of virtual space, each appropriate for different needs, that you can mix and match to produce generative outcomes. She looks at the technical limitations and opportunities of using platforms like Zoom and MS Teams and provides advice for hosting online. The second part (Mastering Virtual Consulting) reflects on being with clients online: the need to adapt 'use of self' and personal presence. Gwen explores how to use virtual opportunities and bypass virtual limitations for things like observing and intervening into group process, coping with the lack of informal interaction, and sensing group energy. A timely book, and one that will likely continue to be relevant when the pandemic is over.

Creating Energized Commitment to the Dialogic Approach: The Change Team's Journey of Discovery

If you want to know how to bring Dialogic OD into an organization that needs it but doesn't know what it is, this is the book you want to read. **Sarah Lewis** brings her considerable experience and intellect to overcoming many of the barriers you will likely encounter when you are the first to use a dialogic, emergent, generative approach. In Dialogic OD, change teams (also known as planning/design teams or steering committees, among other terms) are much, much more than just a group of people planning a project. They are the beginning of change and the key to success. Your expertise in developing a dialogic mindset in the team's members will significantly determine the success of the entire change effort. In this short, lively book, you follow the unfolding interactions with the change sponsor, internal change agent(s), and change team as the OD practitioner lays the essential groundwork for successful organizational transformation.

Initiating and Inviting Generative Change: Entry and Contracting for Emergent Outcomes in Results Driven Organizations.

https://b-m-institute.com/books/initiating-and-inviting-generative-change/

What can you offer and how do you get hired when you can make few promises about what will happen? **Tova Averbuch** provides tested and useful advice on entering and contracting for consulting when the outcomes cannot be predetermined. But this book is much more than that. Tova gives a step-by-step description of a way of being that most professional Dialogic OD practitioners learn only through apprenticeship. She describes how to show up authentically (transparent, expressive, curious) and pull others into a different mindset about leadership and change through one's presence. Tova offers a compelling image of how the Dialogic OD practitioner, through their way of being in covenant relationships, co-creates a network that will enable a large-scale, emergent, generative change process. With numerous real examples, the book illustrates and explains how a consultant enters and establishes an authentic dialogic presence with an ever-expanding group of people, to the point of establishing a planning team that will design the change process.

Change Champions: A Dialogic Approach to Creating an Inclusive Culture

https://b-m-institute.com/books/change_champions-creating-an-inclusive-culture/

For over four decades, **Fred Miller, Monica Biggs, and Judith Katz** have helped organizations, large and small, transform their cultures to be more inclusive and made diversity a strength. In this book, share their experience using "change champions", people from all parts of an organization who volunteer to be advocates for cultural transformation, rapidly changing the core narratives in an organization that shifts day-to-day conversations, actions, and decisions in positive directions. Numerous examples and cases demonstrate the different steps in the unfolding change champion journey to produce a more inclusive organization. This book is a key resource for those wanting to improve inclusion and leverage diversity, equity, and access to achieve higher organizational performance. But this book is more than that, as the change champion method can be adapted for any change requiring an organization-wide shift in thinking and acting. Leaders and professionals who have struggled to increase, for example, safety, sustainability, psychological safety, customer focus, and even cost consciousness may find the change champion approach just what they need to break through the resistance of a strong culture.

Printed in Great Britain
by Amazon

42594163R00069